YORK NOTES

TO KILL A MOCKINGBIRD

HARPER LEE

NOTES BY BETH SIMS

 Longman

 ork Press

YORK PRESS
322 Old Brompton Road, London SW5 9JH

PEARSON EDUCATION LIMITED
Edinburgh Gate, Harlow,
Essex CM20 2JE, United Kingdom
Associated companies, branches and representatives throughout the world

First published 1997
This new and fully revised edition first published 2002
Tenth impression 2009

ISBN: 978-0-582-50628-2

Designed by Michelle Cannatella
Illustrated by Susan Scott
Phototypeset by Gem Graphics, Trenance, Mawgan Porth, Cornwall
Colour reproduction and film output by Spectrum Colour
Produced by Pearson Education Asia Limited, Hong Kong

CONTENTS

PART ONE
INTRODUCTION

PART TWO
SUMMARIES

PART THREE
COMMENTARY

PART FOUR
RESOURCES

PREFACE

York Notes are designed to give you a broader perspective on works of literature studied at GCSE and equivalent levels. With examination requirements changing in the twenty-first century, we have made a number of significant changes to this new series. We continue to help students to reach their own interpretations of the text but York Notes now have important extra-value new features.

You will discover that York Notes are genuinely interactive. The new **Checkpoint** features make sure that you can test your knowledge and broaden your understanding. You will also be directed to excellent websites, books and films where you can follow up ideas for yourself.

The **Resources** section has been updated and an entirely new section has been devoted to how to improve your grade. Careful reading and application of the principles laid out in the Resources section guarantee improved performance.

The **Detailed summaries** include an easy-to-follow skeleton structure of the story-line, while the section on **Language and style** has been extended to offer an in-depth discussion of the writer's techniques.

The Contents page shows the structure of this study guide. However, there is no need to read from the beginning to the end as you would with a novel, play or poem. Use the Notes in the way that suits you. Our aim is to help you with your understanding of the work, not to dictate how you should learn.

Our authors are practising English teachers and examiners who have used their experience to offer a whole range of **Examiner's secrets** – useful hints to encourage exam success.

The General Editor of this series is John Polley, Senior GCSE Examiner and former Head of English at Harrow Way Community School, Andover.

The author of these Notes, Beth Sims, currently works as a freelance editor and writer, after working for seven years in London publishing companies. She has studied English Literature and Language in Nottingham and London. She has taught at school and university level in China, Exeter and London.

The text used in these Notes is the Minerva edition, 1991.

PART ONE

INTRODUCTION

HOW TO STUDY A NOVEL

A novelist starts with a story that examines a situation and the actions of particular characters. Remember that authors are not photographers, and that a novel never resembles real life exactly. Ultimately, a novel represents a view of the world that has been created in the author's imagination.

There are six features of a novel:

❶ THE STORY: this is the series of events, deliberately organised by the writer to test the characters

❷ THE CHARACTERS: the people who have to respond to the events of the story. Since they are human, they can be good or bad, clever or stupid, likeable or detestable, etc. They may change too!

❸ THE VIEWPOINT/VOICE: who is telling the story. The viewpoint may come from one of the characters, or from an omniscient (all-seeing) narrator, which allows the novelist to write about the perspectives of all the characters

❹ THE THEMES: these are the underlying messages, or meanings, of the novel

❺ THE SETTING: this concerns the time and place that the author has chosen for the story

❻ THE LANGUAGE AND STYLE: these are the words that the author has used to influence our understanding of the novel

To arrive at the fullest understanding of a novel, you need to read it several times. In this way, you can see how all the choices the author has made add up to a particular view of life, and develop your own ideas about it.

The purpose of these York Notes is to help you understand what the novel is about and to enable you to make your own interpretation. Do not expect the study of a novel to be neat and easy: novels are chosen for examination purposes, not written for them!

CHECK THE NET
There are literally thousands of websites devoted to Harper Lee and *To Kill a Mockingbird*. To access these websites a useful search engine is **www.google.com**

AUTHOR – LIFE AND WORKS

1926 Harper Lee is born in Monroeville, Alabama, youngest of three children. Her father is a lawyer.

1944–5 Harper Lee attends Huntington College, Montgomery, after attending local schools in Monroeville.

1947–9 Harper Lee studies law at the State University of Alabama.

1950s Harper Lee lives in New York, working as an airline reservations clerk, trying to finance herself as a writer. She eventually gives up this job to work as a writer full-time.

1957 Harper Lee finishes her first draft of *To Kill a Mockingbird*. An editor suggests revisions.

1960 *To Kill a Mockingbird* is published and is an immediate bestseller.

1961 Harper Lee wins the Pulitzer Prize for the novel, and several other awards soon afterwards. 500,000 copies have been sold and the novel translated into ten languages.

1962 *To Kill a Mockingbird* is made into a film, starring Gregory Peck.

Harper Lee continues to live in Monroeville, Alabama, where she moved back to shortly after the publication of her novel. She has published in magazines and journals since writing her bestseller.

CONTEXT

1920s–30s The writer Truman Capote is also brought up in Monroeville, and is a childhood friend of Harper Lee's.

1929 The Great Economic Depression hits the United States (see Setting and Background on p. 7).

1931 The Scottsboro incident occurs where nine black young men are arrested in Scottsboro, Alabama, charged with raping two white women. Some were sentenced to death after several trials (1931-6). Years later it is discovered they are all innocent.

1933 President Roosevelt introduces the New Deal, social and economic policies to try to alleviate poverty and unemployment.

1933 Hitler, leader of the Nazi party, is elected Chancellor of Germany.

1939–45 Second World War

1954 Martin Luther King is working in Montgomery, Alabama, and from here the Black Civil Rights Movement begins, fighting against prejudice, segregation, and for the right to vote.

1956 Montgomery bus boycott where African-Americans try to desegregate town buses.

1956 Autherine Lucy, an African-American woman, attempts to integrate the University of Alabama.

SETTING AND BACKGROUND

To Kill a Mockingbird is set in a small town in Alabama in the Southern States of America (see map on p. 8). Although Maycomb is a fictitious town, based on Harper Lee's home town Monroeville, real places like Montgomery are referred to in the novel. It is useful to consider the context and belief systems of both the time in which it was written (late 1950s) and the era in which it is set (1933–5).

DID YOU KNOW?

All sections of society were hit, because, as Atticus explains to Scout in the novel, professionals depended on their income from farmers who had no money and therefore had to pay them with services instead (p. 23).

1933–5 – Economic depression

- The Wall Street Crash of 1929 caused many shares suddenly to become worthless and poverty swept the country.

- President Roosevelt made substantial attempts at economic recovery. After the National Recovery Act, Roosevelt told the people 'they had nothing to fear but fear itself'. However, these strategies took time to lift the depression.

Late 1950s and Southern American writing

- Black people, who had fought for their country during the Second World War, were starting to demand more civil rights, for instance their right to vote and desegregate. The Black Civil Rights Movement took on a new vigour. Alabama was an important centre in the movement.

- This led to Harper Lee's novel which is a mixture of nostalgia, criticism and perhaps guilt – typical of white Southern American writers of the time who had gained some perspective on the ways of the isolated communities in which they grew up.

Maycomb

Maycomb is a microcosm of American society in the 1930s. It is only concerned with its own problems (of poverty and unemployment) but it is on the eve of major change, both from within and from outside its world. Its geographical position and historical background have shaped its inhabitants – we will see this as we focus on the characters and neighbourhoods of the Maycomb setting. The novel is about one man, Atticus Finch, trying to jolt his society out of this isolationist mentality and towards recognising that black people are humans, who deserve the same rights as white people.

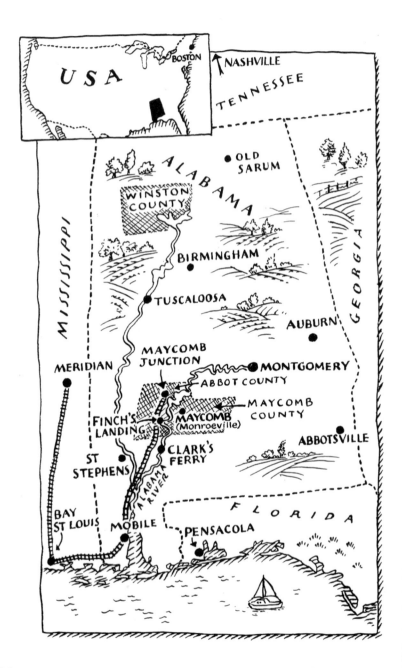

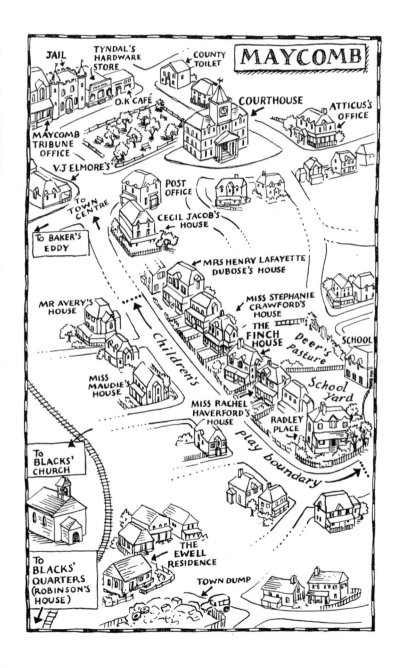

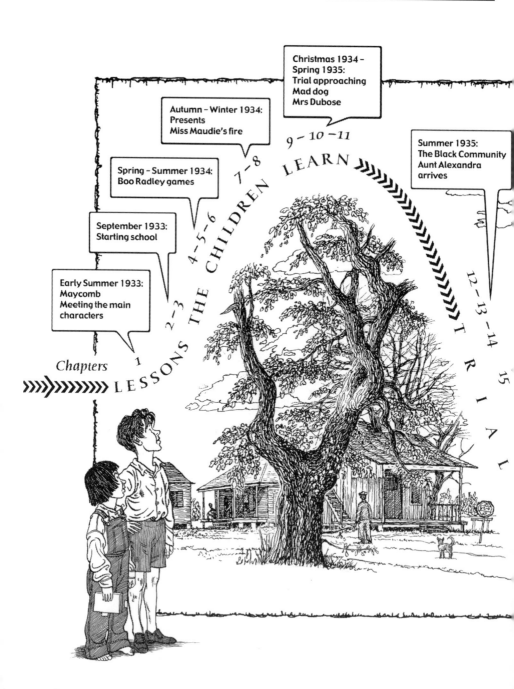

Christmas 1934 –
Spring 1935:
Trial approaching
Mad dog
Mrs Dubose

Autumn – Winter 1934:
Presents
Miss Maudie's fire

Summer 1935:
The Black Community
Aunt Alexandra
arrives

Spring – Summer 1934:
Boo Radley games

September 1933:
Starting school

Early Summer 1933:
Maycomb
Meeting the main
characters

Chapters

1

2–3

4–5–6

7–8

9–10–11

12–13–14

15

LESSONS THE CHILDREN LEARN

TRIAL

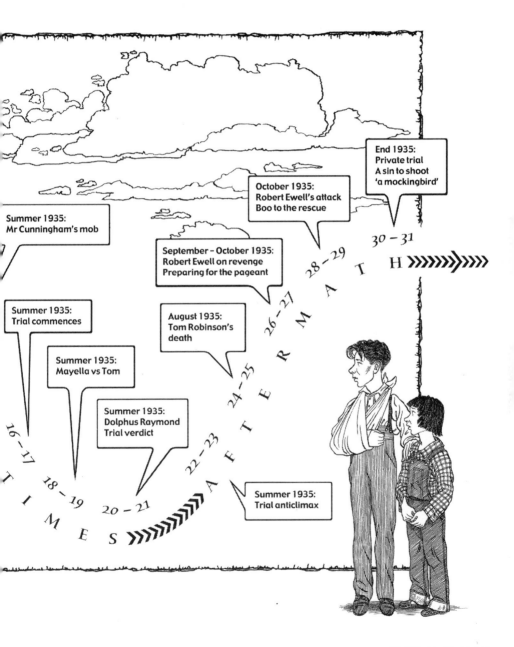

End 1935:
Private trial
A sin to shoot
'a mockingbird'

October 1935:
Robert Ewell's attack
Boo to the rescue

Summer 1935:
Mr Cunningham's mob

September – October 1935:
Robert Ewell on revenge
Preparing for the pageant

30 – 31

28 – 29

26 – 27

H

A

T

Summer 1935:
Trial commences

August 1935:
Tom Robinson's
death

24 – 25

R

M

Summer 1935:
Mayella vs Tom

E

Summer 1935:
Dolphus Raymond
Trial verdict

22 – 23

T

16 – 17

20 – 21

F

18 – 19

Summer 1935:
Trial anticlimax

A

T

I

M

E

S

PART TWO

SUMMARIES

GENERAL SUMMARY

The narrator of the story, Jean-Louise Finch (nicknamed Scout), is looking back at the events of her family life over a period of two and a half years.

CHAPTERS 1–11: LESSONS THE CHILDREN LEARN

DID YOU KNOW?

Harper Lee would have been a similar age to Scout at the time the story is set.

We meet Scout, nearly six, her older brother Jem and friend Dill and their obsessive taunting of reclusive neighbour, Boo Radley. Scout starts school and we learn of the Cunninghams and the Ewells, who are to become key figures later on.

The following summer the plot to make Boo Radley come out of his house resumes. One evening the children are frightened by a shadow and rush to escape; Jem's trousers are torn off and he later finds them repaired and waiting on the fence. During this period, Jem and Scout find presents in a tree beside the Radley Place, and Jem begins to suspect that Boo has left them.

Winter hits Maycomb, Jem and Scout build a snowman and Miss Maudie, a friendly neighbour, has her house burn down. A blanket is placed around Scout's shoulders as she watches the fire, and there is a strong indication that this was done by Boo. The fascination in tormenting Boo decreases.

Scout and Jem learn to be more respectful of their father, particularly after he shoots a mad dog in the street. Atticus has given the children shotguns for Christmas and tells them that it is 'a sin to kill a mockingbird' (Ch. 10, p. 99).

Around this time the children have to learn how to cope with the prejudice directed towards their father by the white community. Atticus, who works as a lawyer in Maycomb, is defending Tom Robinson, a black man. Scout gets into fights and Jem is punished for beheading the flowers of a crabby neighbour.

CHAPTERS 12–21: TRIAL TIMES

The Robinson trial approaches and Jem and Scout learn more about Tom's family and the black community, especially when they are taken to the black church by Calpurnia (the Finch family cook and a surrogate mother for the children). Aunt Alexandra comes to stay with the Finches and her views on black people and bringing up children come into conflict with Atticus's philosophy.

Before the trial Atticus sits outside the door of the Maycomb gaol, guarding Tom Robinson, and a lynch mob threatens. The children appear, looking for their father, and Scout disperses the crowd by her innocent friendliness towards Mr Cunningham.

The trial – Tom Robinson is accused of rape by Mayella Ewell, a poor white girl. Atticus appears to prove Tom's innocence and honest nature. He establishes that Mayella's bruises were the result of blows dealt by a strong left hand. Tom's left hand is crippled. Robert Ewell is ambidextrous and, like his daughter, is shown to be untrustworthy. The watching Jem and Scout are surprised that the white jury find Tom Robinson guilty.

CHAPTERS 22–31: AFTERMATH

Desperate, Tom tries to escape from prison and is shot, before Atticus can bring the case to appeal. Atticus interrupts Aunt Alexandra's missionary tea party for the Maycomb ladies, to ask Calpurnia to accompany him to tell Tom's wife the news of his death.

Mayella's father, Robert Ewell, seeks revenge upon Atticus for their humiliation in court. One evening he attacks Jem and Scout with a knife. Boo Radley comes to the children's aid. Jem is injured and is carried back unconscious to the Finch home by Boo. Robert Ewell is found dead on top of his knife.

Heck Tate, the town sheriff, persuades Atticus to keep the details of the incident quiet, to allow Boo to keep his privacy. Scout finally gets to see Boo and likes what she sees: 'he was real nice' (p. 309). Atticus replies, rounding off the story with the moral lesson that he has reiterated throughout, 'Most people are, Scout, when you finally see them' (p. 309).

 EXAMINER'S SECRET

Although you will rarely have to recount the order of events in an essay, it is useful to remember them, so that you are confident in bringing discussion of the main events into your arguments where relevant.

 DID YOU KNOW?

Atticus's views on black people would have been considered extremely enlightened for the time.

 CHECK THE FILM

When watching the film adaption (directed by Robert Mulligan, 1963) make a note of how far it deviates from the main plot of the novel. Is anything left out or added, and what is the effect of this?

DETAILED SUMMARIES

CHAPTER 1 – When it all began

1 The history of the Finch family, the town of Maycomb and the Radleys (the Finches' neighbours) are described, and the main characters of Jem, Atticus (Scout and Jem's father) and Calpurnia (the Finches' family cook, who helps to bring up the children) are introduced.

2 Jem is ten and Scout six when they meet their next-door neighbour Dill.

3 The children become fascinated with Boo Radley, who has not left his house in fifteen years.

CHECKPOINT 1

How do we know that the narrator is relating to events in the past?

EXAMINER'S SECRET

You will be awarded extra marks if you can use short quotations directly from the novel to back up your points!

We are introduced to the narrative technique that will be used throughout. Scout is the narrator as well as a participant. Events are recounted first-hand, through a child's eyes. However, Scout is also describing events in retrospect; we see the story evolve not only from the fresh viewpoint of a child but also with the hindsight of maturity. We learn of Boo's crimes (pp. 11–12), of the drunken joy-riding and the attack on his father with some scissors, and it is important to consider whether such crimes justify a Radley Place imprisonment.

Note the importance of the Maycomb setting. It is described as if it was a character – old, worn out, unkept, slow-moving, insular, poor, conservative, but also described with hope: 'vague optimism' (p. 6).

Consider the relevance of Roosevelt's comment that people 'had nothing to fear but fear itself' (p. 6) for the Maycomb people and the children.

Note that Calpurnia's comment about a white person is noticed by Scout as being unusual and think about why such caution may be necessary.

Atticus has partly to do the job of both parents as Atticus's wife died when Scout was young. We see that just as Atticus is an individual breaking away from family tradition by setting himself up as a lawyer and leaving the land he also believes in treating his children as individuals.

The factual background information is nicely balanced by the more light-hearted incidents with the children, which help to move the story forward. At this stage, it appears to be a novel about childhood.

CHECK THE BOOK

Encyclopedias such as *The Macmillan Family Encyclopedia* (Macmillan, 1980) will give you information on historical figures and references mentioned in the novel.

Playing boo with Boo

We are taken back to the time when Jem is nearly ten and Scout is nearly six. In the yard of their next-door neighbour, Miss Rachel Haverford, they meet her nephew, Dill, who has come from Mississippi for the summer. The three children, Scout, Jem and Dill become fascinated with the mysterious Boo Radley, who has not left his house in fifteen years. Dill dares Jem to run and knock on the door. Nothing happens, apart from the fact that the children think they see the house shutters move.

This incident is significant as it is the first of many episodes where the children become all-obsessed with Boo.

DID YOU KNOW?

There is a band called 'The Boo Radleys', presumably inspired by Harper Lee's novel.

CHAPTERS 2–3 – An education begins?

1 Scout and Jem begin school, Scout for the first time.

2 Scout's teacher, Miss Caroline Fisher, discovers Scout is bright and scolds her for her advanced learning.

3 Scout returns to school, where Miss Caroline is frightened by Burris Ewell's jumping 'cootie' (Ch. 3, p. 28), and other class members try to explain to her about the Ewell family.

4 When Scout gets home Atticus encourages Scout to look at her experiences in a new light.

> **CHECKPOINT 2**
>
> Who is Scout's most important teacher?

> **CHECKPOINT 3**
>
> How are Miss Caroline's teaching methods different from Atticus's?

> **CHECKPOINT 4**
>
> Is the hairlice incident an effective way to introduce the Ewell family? Why?

 **CHECK THE BOOK**

Hugh Brogan's *Penguin History of the United States of America* (1990) contains useful background information, for instance on the Economic Depression which is very poignant to this novel.

The author is **satirising** education by the careful positioning of ideas (see **Structure**). We are forced to ask ourselves what education is and what its role is.

The impact of the story is heightened by telling it from a child's viewpoint. Whereas Scout is puzzled by Miss Caroline's actions and reactions, the reader has insight into why certain events are occurring and can actually appreciate more than Scout herself.

Flashbacks to past events are often used by the author, for instance Scout telling us that she learned of the Cunninghams from a conversation she overheard last year. This makes the story **realistic** as a past and a future are implied as well as a present. The novel is in fact one large flashback.

Note the reference to poverty (Ch. 2, p. 23) – particularly for those who owned or worked on farms – as the price of cotton had fallen significantly following the Economic Depression (see **Setting and background**).

Walter's country ways and dialect are different from the Finches'. A barrier of class has been broken down here.

Jem's definition of 'entailment' (Ch. 2, p. 23) is an example of **malapropism** which is a common technique used by the author for creating humour (see **Language and style**).

Scout learns a lesson from Calpurnia on social manners. At the same time the author is able to point out a moral to the reader, a technique frequently used. The same technique is employed when Atticus tells Scout that you cannot fully understand someone until you look at things from his/her point of view, 'his skin' (Ch. 3, p. 33). This is a key concept in the novel.

By making Miss Caroline a naive outsider, the author has an opportunity to acquaint the reader with Maycomb's inhabitants. We learn about the background of the Ewell and Cunningham families, which we need to know for later. We see how close-knit the Maycomb community is when the children are able to stereotype and make generalisations about particular groups of people that Miss Caroline, from North Alabama, cannot understand.

Social manners

When Scout's fellow pupil, Walter Cunningham, refuses to borrow money from Miss Caroline to buy some lunch, Miss Caroline will not accept the refusal. Scout tries to explain Walter Cunningham's behaviour and is consequently punished. Scout is angry and attempts a fight with Walter Cunningham in the playground. Jem stops this and invites Walter back to the Finches' for lunch. Calpurnia scolds Scout for commenting on Walter's table manners.

CHECK THE BOOK

Black Like Me (1960) is a true story told by John Howard Griffin, who disguises himself as a black man to experience what this is like in late 1950s southern America.

DID YOU KNOW?

Note that there are no black children at Scout's school.

GLOSSARY

entailment a legal process where a person has the use of land without being the owner of it

cootie body/headlice

Now take a break!

CHAPTERS 4–6 – The fascination continues

❶ Scout and Jem discover gifts hidden in an oak tree, and start to wonder who has left them there.

❷ Scout rolls in a tyre, pushed by Jem, into the Radley steps.

❸ The children take on character roles – Dill's 'worst performance was Gothic' (Ch. 4, p. 43) – in a Boo Radley play and are caught by Atticus but deny the Radley connection.

❹ Scout spends time with Miss Maudie, a kindly neighbour, who tells her more about the Radley family.

❺ The children leave Boo a note and Atticus catches them, asking them how they would feel if he entered their bedrooms without knocking.

CHECKPOINT 5

Why are Atticus's words so effective? What earlier quotation does this remind you of?

The children are part of a mob (see Chapter 16). When Scout is rejected by the mob she experiences a sense of isolation and has to acquire an individual's perspective.

We see what a fair person Atticus is. Even though he suspects that the children's game is to do with the Radleys, because they deny it and he has no proof, he lets it go – perhaps this behaviour is more representative of a lawyer than most parents. How believable is Atticus's behaviour? Is he just too good to be true?

We learn more about the Radleys from Miss Maudie, giving us an alternative perspective about Boo Radley than that built up by the children. In contrast, Boo's mystery persona is built up further by the children.

EXAMINER'S SECRET

Keep a note of where important concepts are repeated, perhaps using slightly different language. These concepts reveal important messages of the novel.

Despite Scout being the narrator, it seems she does not fully understand the implications of her conversations with Miss Maudie. Scout thinks that Miss Maudie is accusing Atticus of drinking whisky. Miss Maudie's conversation with Miss Stephanie (Ch. 5, pp. 50–1) is also misunderstood. As well as showing Scout's innocence, this becomes an opportunity for humour. It creates the effect of removing an omniscience from the narrator, just because s/he knows more than the reader. She in fact knows less. Readers therefore, aware of the gap of understanding, must frequently make sense of things for themselves.

The neighbours presume that the intruder in Mr Radley's yard is 'a Negro' (Ch 6, p. 60). Black people were often scapegoats, automatically linked with crimes. This fear and paranoia is also reflected by people's response to Boo Radley in Maycomb (see **Theme** on **Prejudice**). As we learn in Chapter 1 'Any stealthy crimes committed in Maycomb were his work' (p. 9).

EXAMINER'S SECRET
Consider how this novel is different from other works that you are studying with **first-person narration**. The examiner will be impressed if you can make comparisons and contrasts with other works.

EXAMINER'S SECRET
It is useful to make note of how the writer uses language to build up atmosphere, as well as just remembering the plot, as this will be useful in essays. For instance, look at the description of the Radley Place on pp. 58–9 and consider how the sinister mood is built up.

Jem loses his trousers

On the last night of the summer holidays the children go towards the Radley house to look through their shutters, following rules of superstitious behaviour to protect themselves (Ch. 6, p. 58). As Jem approaches the steps a shadow crosses him and the children run away. Jem catches his trousers on the fence and rips them off as a sound of a gun shot is heard. Later that night Jem returns to fetch his trousers from the Radleys' fence, as he is more scared of being punished by Atticus in the morning should his trousers be lost than he is of the Nathan Radley gun. As he tells Scout in Chapter 7, he finds that they have been roughly mended and folded and placed back on the fence.

This action will force the children to consider Boo as a real person.

GLOSSARY
Gothic a type of nineteenth-century literature which emphasised the horrific and paranormal

CHAPTERS 7–8 – Everyone to help

① Jem and Scout find more things in the tree knot-hole.

② The children try to leave a thank-you letter, and discover Mr Nathan Radley, Boo's keeper, filling up the hole.

CHECKPOINT 6

Consider Mr Nathan's action. This is the first time in the novel something innocent is being harmed unnecessarily. Why is he doing this?

③ A cold winter brings heavy snow to Maycomb, as heavy as the 'Appomattox' (Ch. 8, p. 72) according to Mr Avery. Scout and Jem's snowman is 'an absolute morphodite' (Miss Maudie, Ch. 8, p. 75).

④ Miss Maudie's house catches fire. As Jem and Scout watch, Boo, unnoticed by the children, places a blanket around Scout's shoulders.

⑤ Jem realises who has put it there and pours out to Atticus all the events concerning Boo. Initially, Scout does not understand why.

The difference of age and understanding between Jem and Scout is brought out clearly (see **Theme** on **Growing up**). We see Jem slowly puzzling out Mr Nathan's action and that it is Boo who has left these gifts, and also that it is Boo who has put the blanket around Scout's shoulders. Scout comments on Jem but not does not understand his line of thought.

Courage (a recurring theme of the novel) and humour are shown the day after the house fire, when Miss Maudie says, 'Always wanted a smaller house, Jem Finch. Gives me more yard' (Ch. 8, p. 80).

CHAPTERS 9–11 – A sin to kill a mockingbird

EXAMINER'S SECRET

You will recognise that part of the quotation on p. 99 forms the novel's title, and that therefore it is important. Keep a note of it and as you are reading consider its significance.

① Atticus has taken on a court-case and is defending a 'Negro' (Ch. 9, p. 83) called Tom Robinson.

② The children must learn self-control to accusations of their father, for instance at school and at Finch's Landing, where they are spending Christmas with Aunt Alexandra and other family.

③ The children are given air rifles for Christmas. Atticus says, 'Shoot all the bluejays you want, if you can hit 'em, but remember it's a sin to kill a mockingbird' (Ch. 9, p. 99).

4 Jem knocks the heads off Mrs Dubose's camellias after she has shouted vicious things out about Atticus.

5 As a punishment from Atticus he is forced to read to Mrs Dubose every night.

6 Before her death she leaves a single white camellia for Jem. Scout and Jem learn that Mrs Dubose had been cantankerous as she had been fighting a morphine addiction.

7 Atticus tells the children that 'I wanted you to see what real courage is, instead of getting the idea that courage is a man with a gun in his hand' (Ch. 11, p. 124).

CHECKPOINT 7

What could this flower-gift symbolise?

 DID YOU KNOW?

Although Mrs Dubose is not a 'nigger-lover' herself, the **irony** is how dependent she is on her 'Negress' servant Jessie! This would have been a very common relationship in the 1930s.

 EXAMINER'S SECRET

The theme of courage is a strong one in the novel. Build up quotes under main theme headings. This will make life easier for you when you revise and write essays.

We are introduced to Tom Robinson when Atticus tells Scout that he has taken on a 'peculiar case' (Ch. 9, p. 83). Before we learn too much about this, we hear that Calpurnia has said that 'they're clean living folks' (Ch. 9, p. 83). Atticus respects Calpurnia, and as we have been encouraged to respect both characters, this directs positive feelings towards Tom Robinson who, up to now, we know little about.

Through Scout's experiences with Uncle Jack and Aunt Alexandra, we see the message coming across (which Scout has learned from Atticus – see Chapter 4) that it is important to hear two sides of an argument and to have proof and not to make assumptions.

GLOSSARY
Appomattox the last battle of the Civil War; when the Southerners were finally defeated
absolute morphodite hermaphrodites have both male and female characteristics, in this instance resembling both Mr Avery and Miss Maudie

Chapters 9–11 continued

In the description of Atticus at the beginning of Chapter 10 we learn that he has a problem with his left eye. This disability links Atticus to Tom Robinson with his crippled left arm. Atticus, in the children's opinion and before they learn to appreciate his other qualities, is not 'macho' enough compared to other fathers. This relates to Harper Lee's breaking down of the stereotype of the Southern Gentleman (see **Theme** on **Prejudice**).

One-Shot Finch

CHECKPOINT 8
Why is a first-hand account effective here?

A mad dog is spotted in the street (Chapter 10). Calpurnia phones for the town sheriff, Heck Tate, and Atticus, and makes sure all the neighbours stay in their houses. Heck Tate hands the gun to Atticus, and in one shot the dog is dead. Scout and Jem had previously wondered what special skills their father had and had noticed that he did not do the things their contemporaries' fathers did. Now Scout and Jem learn something new about their father and their respect for him increases. It is a crucial time to have gained the children's respect – just before the trial days begin.

Zeebo comes to collect the mad dog (Chapter 10) as his job is the local garbage collector. We learn (Chapter 12) that he is one of the few black people there who can read. This tells us a lot about the position of black people in society and their job opportunities.

CHECKPOINT 9
What does the incident with the mad dog **symbolise** (see **Theme** on **Symbolism**)?

Scout's overhearing of Jack and Atticus speaking helps the reader learn first-hand how Atticus feels about the trial, as does Scout observing Jem's punishment. Scout is given a reason for eavesdropping (to listen if Uncle Jack is telling on her) and for accompanying Jem to visit Mrs Dubose (her devotion to Jem). However if Scout were to be present too often, we would become too aware of authorial purpose and the story might seem contrived.

WHO SAYS ...?

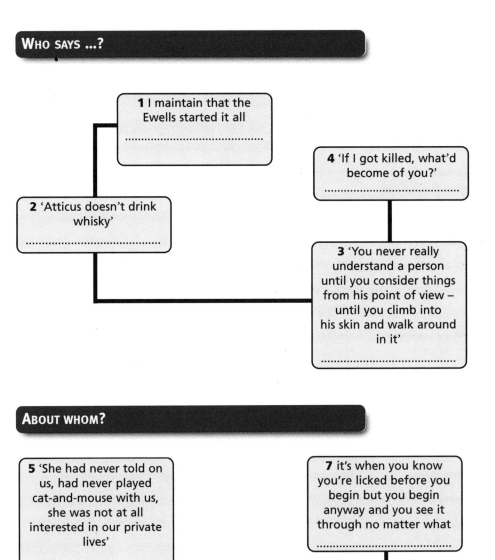

1 I maintain that the Ewells started it all

....

4 'If I got killed, what'd become of you?'

....

2 'Atticus doesn't drink whisky'

....

3 'You never really understand a person until you consider things from his point of view – until you climb into his skin and walk around in it'

....

ABOUT WHOM?

5 'She had never told on us, had never played cat-and-mouse with us, she was not at all interested in our private lives'

....

7 it's when you know you're licked before you begin but you begin anyway and you see it through no matter what

....

6 'he dined on raw squirrels and any cats he could catch'

....

Check your answers on p. 81.

CHAPTERS 12–14 – Gentle breeding

❶ Calpurnia takes Jem and Scout to the black people's church, and we learn about Tom Robinson's family and that he is accused of rape.

❷ Aunt Alexandra has come to stay. She persuades Atticus to try to make Jem and Scout appreciate that 'you are not from run-of-the-mill people' (Ch. 13, p. 147).

❸ Aunt Alexandra and Atticus quarrel about Calpurnia's position in the household.

❹ Dill turns up, having run away from his home in Mississippi.

It is appropriate that one episode (Chapter 12) should take place in a church as we have previously learned that all the main events of Maycomb are centred around church activities. In this chapter we find out much more about the black community of Maycomb, their community care, their dignity and also the Tom Robinson family.

Lula May is the only black character with any 'negative' characteristics. Critics have said the lack of such characters makes the novel unrealistic. However, at the time black people could not show their disapproval of white ways, for fear of prejudice and losing their jobs. Therefore perhaps it is realistic that black discontent can only be shown to a child who is breaking the rules of segregation that have been imposed on the black people by the white people.

Read the description of Maycomb as an 'inward' (Ch. 13, p. 144) town. It may be difficult to affect change in such a community.

It is **ironic** that Aunt Alexandra wants the children to appreciate their background, characterised as it was by enslavement, when it is the freedom of black Tom Robinson that Atticus is fighting for. The children know little about the Finch family and we get the impression that Atticus does not wish them to know their links with the past. They should form their own views about the world and not take on family airs and graces. Even though Atticus is a lawyer, he is ineffective at putting his heart into saying something that he does not believe in. This contrasts with his passion and conviction in the forthcoming trial.

CHECKPOINT 10

Why are Jem and Scout disappointed and confused at Atticus's talk?

EXAMINER'S SECRET

Think about how and when the author presents information to the reader. For instance we have heard only positive things about Tom Robinson and negative things about the Ewells, so therefore we are naturally more inclined to sympathise with Tom Robinson before the trial even begins.

Jem is growing up

In Chapter 14 Jem tells Scout what to do and the next moment he starts fighting with her and Atticus has to intervene. Later in this chapter Jem goes to tell Atticus about Dill's arrival. This depicts his different adult and childlike phases as he is growing up (see **Theme** on **Growing up**).

CHAPTER 15 – Calming the mob

1 Heck Tate, the sheriff, tells Atticus they are moving Tom Robinson to the local gaol and warns of trouble with 'that Old Sarum bunch' (p. 160). Atticus disappears the next night and the children follow.

2 They find Atticus outside the gaol and a gang gathers around him.

3 Scout makes a speech directed towards Mr Cunningham about his 'entailment' (p. 169) and about his son.

4 Mr Cunningham disperses the crowd and they leave.

We see how the innocence of a child can disperse a group of angry men by inadvertently appealing to their humanity, saving Atticus from a potentially nasty situation. Scout is unconsciously pointing out a moral to them, that it is a sin to kill a mockingbird (Atticus/Tom Robinson).

As Atticus points out to Scout later, people's behaviour changes when they are part of a mob. Note that Atticus is always shown on his own, never as part of a group. He does not seem to need other people to back up his opinions.

Note the description of the gaol in this chapter (p. 165) and the description of the court-house in Chapter 16 (p. 179) and consider whether these descriptions **symbolise** what goes on in the buildings.

CHECKPOINT 11

How does Scout learn about the information Heck Tate tells Atticus?

 CHECK THE BOOK

Truman Capote also wrote about a child growing up in the Southern States of America in roughly the same period. See *Other Voices, Other Rooms*.

CHAPTERS 16–17 –The trial begins

1 It is the day of the trial.

2 Atticus speaks to Scout about last night's proceedings, explaining that Mr Cunningham is a friend, but that he has faults like everyone else and that last night he was part of a mob.

3 People from all around Maycomb are arriving for the trial.

4 In the court-house the children cannot find anywhere to sit, until Reverend Sykes offers them seats in the 'Coloured balcony' (Ch. 16, p. 181).

5 The trial begins with Mr Heck Tate's testimony. He attests that Mayella's right eye was badly bruised.

CHECKPOINT 12

Note the reference again to standing in another's shoes. Who stood? Whose shoes?

 DID YOU KNOW?

Town trials were big social events in the 1930s.

It was important that Dill came back on the scene at the end of Chapter 14. His purpose here is to get information to the reader about the people coming to the trial, as it was earlier to learn of the Radleys and Maycomb. Jem tells Dill about the various well-known characters, for example Mr Dolphus Raymond, shunned by the white community for living with and having children by a black woman and being permanently drunk from whisky. Miss Maudie says she is not attending the 'carnival' (Ch. 16, p. 176).

Look at Scout's remark, 'Well if we came out durin' the Old Testament it's too long ago to matter' (Ch. 16, p. 178) in the context of the conversation about whether they could have black ancestors. Note that although the children are not racially prejudiced in a blatantly conventional way, they have still picked up some of the beliefs and definitions from their community. This includes their view of Dolphus Raymond, which is necessary information for the encounter with him later.

The segregation between the black people and white people is emphasised by the way the black people file in last and are seated in the balcony. Their kindly politeness to Jem, Scout and Dill is again shown when four black people give up their front seats for the three of them! This also implies that white children have precedence over black adults. It is ironic that the children will have the same viewpoint as them in the trial – in terms of what they see and where they see it from.

Compare the description of the Ewells' place of living with the Negroes' houses (Ch. 17, pp. 187–8) and think what effect this is designed to have upon you as reader and what these settings tell you about character.

Questioning Robert Ewell

Mr Gilmer (who is presenting Mayella Ewell against Tom Robinson) questions Robert Ewell, who is provoked into such bad language that the court proceedings are interrupted. Note his lack of understanding of general language like 'ambidextrous' (Ch. 17, p. 196), in contrast to Scout, who uses legal language very comfortably, e.g. 'circuit solicitor' (Ch. 17, p. 183), to discuss court proceedings. Atticus cross-questions Robert Ewell who agrees that it was Mayella's right eye that was bruised, and reveals his left-handedness to the court. Jem believes the case is won, but Scout is not so sure – Tom Robinson could be left-handed too.

DID YOU KNOW?

It is perhaps ironic that Robert Ewell as a white man is asked to prove his literacy, and that this act of writing with his left hand hints at his guilt and Tom's innocence, while in slave times if it was discovered that a black man could write he was punished and sometimes his right hand was cut off.

GLOSSARY

ambidextrous the ability to use both hands equally well

circuit solicitor a lawyer who works within a defined area

CHAPTERS 18–19 – Mayella vs Tom

❶ Mayella Ewell is questioned by Mr Gilmer and then by Atticus – she has problems answering questions.

❷ Attticus asks Mayella to be sure she has got the right man and she gets confused, before eventually bursting into tears for the second time and refusing to say more.

❸ Jem notices that Tom has a withered left hand at the end of a crippled left arm.

❹ Tom Robinson takes the stand and Atticus questions him on his version of events, after which Mr Gilmer questions him (see below).

❺ Mr Link Deas, who used to employ Tom, speaks for his defence out of turn ('*ex cathedra* remarks', Ch. 19, p. 216) and is sent out of the room, adding to the courtroom drama.

We see the discrepancies between Mayella and Tom's stories. Notice where the 'chiffarobe' appears in the two versions. It is clear that Tom would not say that he had helped Mayella previously if he had not, as it would do nothing to help his case – Mayella had stated that this was the first time she had called for his help.

EXAMINER'S SECRET

See how the author makes a judgement about characters without being overt, just by the use of their language.

Notice the polite language that Tom uses, not wishing to reiterate in court Robert Ewell's bad language (Ch. 19, p. 215), and not wishing to say that Mayella is lying but repeating 'she's mistaken in her mind' (Ch. 19, p. 218). Mayella in contrast does not understand Atticus's polite language and when he calls her 'Ma'am' says to Judge Taylor 'I don't hafta take his sass' (Ch. 18, p. 200). Mr Gilmer doesn't accord the same respect when he is questioning Tom, addressing him patronisingly as 'boy' (Ch. 19, p. 218).

You felt sorry for her

Mr Gilmer questions Tom and asks him why he did odd jobs for Mayella for no money. Tom states that he saw that she was struggling and that Mr Ewell and the children weren't any help and that he felt 'sorry' for her. Mr Gilmer picks up on this, stating, '*You* felt sorry for *her*, you felt *sorry* for her?' (Ch. 19, p. 218).

CHECKPOINT 13

Why does Tom's admittance of sympathy for Mayella spell doom for him?

CHAPTERS 20—1 – The verdict

1 Scout has left the court-house with Dill, as he is feeling unwell. They meet and talk to Dolphus Raymond.

2 Dill and Scout return to the court-room to hear Atticus conclude his defence of Tom Robinson. He appeals to the jury, 'This case is as simple as black and white' (Ch. 20, p. 224).

3 Several hours later, the jury present the verdict: Tom Robinson is guilty.

4 The black people stand as Atticus files out of the court-room.

Note Mr Raymond's use of the phrase 'run-of-the-mill' (Ch. 20, p. 222) in contrast to Aunt Alexandra's use of it (Ch. 13, p. 147).

CHECKPOINT 14

What is Atticus implying by this statement?

CHECKPOINT 15

Consider how many winning points Mr Gilmer makes compared to Atticus, and Mayella makes compared to Tom in the trial scenes.

The theme about the innocence of children, who have not been effected by society's prejudices and therefore can only judge things by natural justice, is also referred to by Atticus after the Cunningham mob scene and later as they discuss the trial. Look at these examples (Ch. 16, p. 173 and Ch. 22, p. 235). Consider the importance for Harper Lee of getting across this statement, when her **epigraph** is 'Lawyers, I suppose, were children once' (Charles Lamb). Also think about whether this is a contradiction in the novel, as the children do show prejudice towards Boo Radley.

GLOSSARY

ex cathedra remarks comments which should not strictly be part of court proceedings

chiffarobe wardrobe

take his sass accept his insult

Meeting Dolphus Raymond

The interlude with Dolphus Raymond gives the reader a breathing space from the intensity of the trial and foreshadows Atticus's views, expressed later, that black people are people like everyone else. This scene underlines the prejudices of the white community, hinting that if a white person loves a black person they have to have an excuse for it and Scout learns more about the 'simple hell people give other people' (Ch. 20, p. 222). Dolphus Raymond's 'perpetrated fraud' (Ch. 20, p. 221) is one way in which society copes with threats to its established norms. Mayella's guilty denial could be seen as another.

CHECKPOINT 16

What is the 'perpetrated fraud'?

Now take a break!

TEST YOURSELF (CHAPTERS 12–21)

WHO SAYS ...?

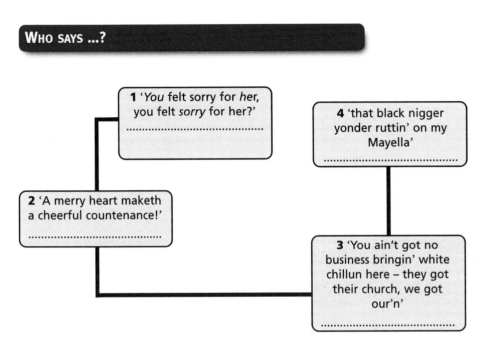

1 '*You* felt sorry for *her*, you felt *sorry* for her?'
....

4 'that black nigger yonder ruttin' on my Mayella'
....

2 'A merry heart maketh a cheerful countenance!'
....

3 'You ain't got no business bringin' white chillun here – they got their church, we got our'n'
....

ABOUT WHOM?

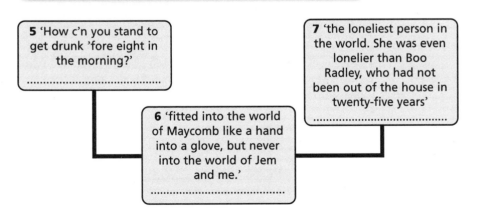

5 'How c'n you stand to get drunk 'fore eight in the morning?'
....

7 'the loneliest person in the world. She was even lonelier than Boo Radley, who had not been out of the house in twenty-five years'
....

6 'fitted into the world of Maycomb like a hand into a glove, but never into the world of Jem and me.'
....

Check your answers on p. 81.

CHAPTERS 22–3 – Following the trial

1 Jem is very upset by the trial result, Aunt Alexandra wondering if it was a good idea to allow the children to be present. Atticus believes that they must get used to the society in which they live.

2 Atticus, very tired, wakes up to find that many black people have left him gifts of food and he is moved to tears.

3 Miss Maudie tries to offer support to the children and discusses the trial with them. She has only made two little cakes instead of her usual three for Jem, Scout and Dill. Scout realises why when Miss Maudie cuts a slice from the big cake for Jem.

4 Chapter 23 is concluded when Jem tells Scout that he has been thinking that there are four types of people in the world whereas Scout disagrees, saying that there is only one.

CHECKPOINT 17

Look at Scout and Jem's different views. What are the four and what is the one? Which views do you agree with most?

CHECKPOINT 18

What does Atticus's language remind you of?

Atticus's words to Jem about the trial are strong, his outrage revealed. Although the effect on the reader is powerful, when looking closely at Atticus's words we see how even a very unusually enlightened man of his time is affected by the standard 'white' perception of black people and, however sympathetic and tolerant, cannot completely step into a black man's skin (see **Theme** on **Prejudice**). He tells Jem, 'There's nothing more sickening to me than a low-grade white man who'll take advantage of a Negro's ignorance' (Ch. 23, p. 243). This view of black ignorance was common in the white world at the time. But a white man can take advantage of a black man in other ways than ignorance. Therefore such words, from a modern perspective, are not so politically correct.

See how difficult it is for Atticus to explain society's prejudice to the children and how he resorts to only a partial explanation – that it is due to the inadequacies of the legal system.

Note the language that Atticus uses to Jem: '*You* couldn't, but *they* could' (Ch. 23, p. 243). See the definition of **leitmotif**

Atticus seems too optimistic in his view of the people of Maycomb (Ch. 23, p. 241), and this echoes how he was before the incident with the Cunningham mob. Because this mirrors earlier patterns of misplaced optimism (Chapter 15), like Scout and Jem we feel apprehensive again.

Note how Atticus uses the word 'trash' (Ch. 23, p. 243) and how different Aunt Alexandra's definition of this word is (Ch. 23, p. 248).

Atticus discusses the trial

Bob Ewell spits in Atticus's face and tells him he will seek revenge, even if it takes the rest of his life. The children worry about their father's safety. Atticus tries to make the children stand in 'Bob Ewell's shoes' (Ch. 23, p. 241) and reassures them that they are quite safe. He talks more with the children about the trial (note his ready use of legal language like 'commutes his sentence', 'straight acquittal' and 'hung jury', Ch. 23, pp. 241–6), and about prejudice against black people. He tells the children that a Cunningham on the jury, who had previously been connected with the potential lynch mob outside the gaol, had been convinced by Atticus's arguments that Tom Robinson was innocent and had initially stood for an acquittal.   ctd ...

CHECKPOINT 19

What is Atticus trying to get the children to do again? Look at your previous examples of this key statement about other people's shoes.

GLOSSARY

commutes his sentence reduces the severity of his sentence
straight acquittal immediate release
hung jury where the jury cannot reach a clear decision acceptable for sentencing i.e. two dissenters out of twelve

CHECK THE BOOK

The final chapter of *Black Like Me* (1960) by John Howard Griffin, documents race relations in the Civil Rights Movement. For historical documents of the Scottsboro Trials and the Civil Rights Movement check out *Understanding To Kill a Mockingbird* by Claudia Durst Johnson (1994).

Atticus's statement about a Cunningham could be considered one of the most optimistic notes of the novel, along with the jury taking a long time to reach their verdict and Mr Underwood's newspaper article. Atticus has managed to make another man, from a racist, traditional white family, stop and think for a moment. However, Atticus is a man of his time. He cannot let go of his slightly patronising and paternalistic view – that the racial issue will only be solved by white people changing their attitudes. The later Civil Rights Movement (see **Author and context**) was mainly initiated by, and for, black people.

CHAPTERS 24–5 – Tom's death

1 Aunt Alexandra is entertaining the Maycomb Missionary Society and they have an interesting discussion about race, which Miss Maudie angrily brings to an end.

2 Atticus comes home with the news that Tom Robinson is dead and he asks Calpurnia to accompany him to go and tell Helen, Tom's wife.

CHECKPOINT 20

Why do you think the songbird theme recurs again here?

3 Mr Underwood reports the death in the *Maycomb Tribune*, likening it to 'the senseless slaughter of songbirds' (Ch. 25, p. 265).

Note the irony of the ladies' conversation when there are black people in their own society living in similar conditions. Harper Lee brings this to the reader's attention by Mrs Merriweather's use of alliteration of 'sin and squalor' (Ch. 24, p. 255) which is repeated for effect.

The news of Tom's death arrives during the missionary ladies' tea party, making their talk seem trivial compared to the realities of the outside world. (See **Structure** for comments on purposeful juxtaposition of events.) The author seems to be echoing Scout's thought when she comments, 'I was more at home in my father's world' (Ch. 24, p. 258).

We see from such a scene with the missionary ladies that it is perhaps necessary to have idealised black characters. Any bad (human?) traits, like the sulking of the black community following the trial, seem to be seized upon by the white community. Perhaps Harper Lee was aware of such attitudes in wider society and therefore made a conscious effort to focus on the good in the black characters.

Although we learned from the lynch mob incident outside the gaol that Mr Underwood 'despises Negroes' (Ch. 16, p. 172) we also learned and see again now from his reaction to Tom's death that he despises injustice. This is a curious mixture of characteristics and suggests that the characters which Harper Lee portrays are complex.

Messengers of bad news

Jem and Dill accompany Atticus and Calpurnia to the Quarters. Dill tells Scout about their trip to tell the Robinsons of Tom's death. This is one of the few scenes in the novel where Scout is not present. The incident at the Robinsons' home is instead recounted as Scout remembers what Dill told her. Dill tells Scout of Helen falling when she learns of her husband's death – 'like a giant with a big foot just came along and stepped on her' (Ch. 25, pp. 264–5). Consider the effectiveness of this simile (see **Language and style**).

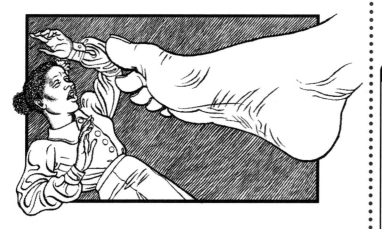

CHECKPOINT 21

Look at this passage and consider whether it is as effective as the incidents that Scout recounts herself. Is it as immediate and vivid to the reader as **first-person narrative**?

CHAPTERS 26–7 – A score to settle

❶ The school year begins again and Scout is surprised when Miss Gates, her teacher, talks about Hitler's persecution of the Jews, contrasting it to the non-prejudiced United States.

❷ Scout cannot understand Miss Gates as she heard her putting down black people to Miss Stephanie, as she came out of the court-house.

❸ Jem shouts at Scout not to talk of the court-house again, and Atticus later explains to the puzzled Scout that Jem needs to forget about the trial incident for a while.

❹ Robert Ewell has not forgotten that he has a score to settle. At the Welfare Office he complains, quite unreasonably, of Atticus stealing his job.

❺ Judge Taylor's house is broken into, probably by Robert Ewell, and Helen Robinson is threatened by Robert Ewell.

❻ Mr Link Deas, who has given Helen work, has to warn Ewell to leave her alone.

CHECKPOINT 22
Look back to the trial scenes and consider whether you agree with this statement about the judge.

Atticus explains to Aunt Alexandra, who is worried about his safety after the incidents with Robert Ewell, that Robert Ewell had tried to burgle the judge's house because the judge had made him 'look like a fool' in the trial (Ch. 27, p. 276).

See how Misses Tutti and Frutti blame the unknown outsider (see **Theme** on **Prejudice**) for stealing their missing furniture.

Aunt Alexandra has a premonition before the pageant (Ch. 27, p. 279) as Jem did before the mob scene (Ch. 15, p. 164).

Maycomb returns to normality

After the events of the trial, Maycomb returns to normality and Scout reports incidents such as the prank of the local children moving the furniture from Misses Tutti and Frutti Barbers' house to the cellar. At Halloween a pageant is organised by Mrs Merriweather and the Maycomb ladies and Scout is given the part of a 'Pork' (Ch. 27, p. 279). Scout performs her part at home to Atticus, Aunt Alexandra and Cal and heads off to the pageant with Jem, beginning their 'longest journey together' (Ch. 27, p. 280 – see foreshadowing). Such 'normal' events are important in a novel with a documentary as well as a dramatic purpose (see realism), and a time of calm is necessary after the pace and tension of the trial chapters.

CHECKPOINT 23

In what general ways could Mrs Merriweather be likened to Harper Lee?

CHAPTERS 28–9 – Attacked in the dark

1 Jem and Scout walk to the pageant in the dark and Cecil Jacobs, from Scout's class, jumps out on them.

2 Scout falls asleep waiting for her line in the pageant, causing her so much embarrassment that she decides to stay inside her costume until she gets home.

3 Jem leads Scout back in the dark, and they hear noises behind them. They think it must be Cecil following them at first, until the supposed prank carries on too long.

4 Somebody attacks Scout, there is a big scuffle and she hears strange noises from beneath her costume. She hears a 'crunching sound' (Ch. 28, p. 289) and Jem screams.

CHECKPOINT 24

What is the 'crunching'?

5 As Scout reels from a blow she hears a man wheeze then cough and stagger away groaning. Scout then finds a man on the ground who smells of whisky and a man carries Jem back to the Finch home.

6 Heck Tate arrives and says that he has found Bob Ewell dead under the Radleys' tree, with a knife in his ribs. Heck Tate asks Scout to tell him what happened.

7 At the end of her story she points to the man in the corner who

came to their rescue and she realises this man is Boo.

A feeling of suspense is created through the use of language in

Chapter 28. The reference to the 'solitary mocker' (Ch. 28, p. 281) at the beginning of the chapter **foreshadows** the mockingbird (Boo) appearing later.

The incident with Cecil jumping out on Jem and Scout is timely, as the reader expects danger but it turns out to be a prank. The author is cleverly building up the parallels, for instance one of the pageant stalls consisted of the unseeing children being made to touch imaginary parts of a human (see **Structure**). Thus when the Robert Ewell episode occurs later, the climax is even more dramatic and sinister in contrast.

Note that Aunt Alexandra dresses Scout in her tomboy clothes in which she will be comfortable following the disturbing incident with Robert Ewell. At important times like these Aunt Alexandra forgets her strife to make Scout into a lady.

CHECKPOINT 25

What does such an act make us feel towards Aunt Alexandra?

CHAPTERS 30–1 – A private trial

1. Doctor Reynolds arrives and asks everyone to leave the room while he examines Jem.

2. Atticus, Heck Tate, Arthur (Boo) Radley and Scout go out onto the porch. Scout leads Boo into a seat in a shadow as she senses that he will be more comfortable there.

3. Atticus discusses the incident with Heck Tate. Atticus does not understand why Heck is insisting that Bob Ewell fell on his knife and believes that the incident must come to court, even though it would be difficult for Jem.

4. He eventually understands that Heck is trying to protect Boo Radley's privacy.

5. Scout takes Boo Radley in to see Jem who is asleep, and then, at Boo's request, walks him home, the last she will see of him.

6. As Scout walks home she looks back at the incidents that have happened from Boo's viewpoint and contemplates Atticus's moral of seeing things as if standing in another's shoes.

7. Scout joins Atticus beside the sleeping Jem and very soon after Atticus begins to read her *'The Grey Ghost'* (Ch. 31, p. 309) she has fallen asleep.

Although we suspect it was Boo, we are not certain whether it was Jem or Boo who stabbed Bob Ewell with his knife. Harper Lee implies that this is not the real issue here, but instead the importance of protecting an innocent creature (Boo) from society. Atticus is persuaded by Heck that the public's legal system is not suitable here, that they must judge the system by their own rules and sense of justice. The legal system was not sufficient to save the other mockingbird of the story. We do not know whether Scout has completely understood Atticus and Heck's conversation, or whether she has just responded to Heck Tate's repetition of the word 'sin' and linked it with Atticus's lesson in Chapter 10 when the mockingbird is first introduced. But her words are poignant when she says that if the incident was exposed to the public 'it'd be sort of like shootin' a mockingbird' (Ch. 30, p. 304).

Heck Tate employs as evidence Bob Ewell's left-handedness (Ch.30, p. 302)

CHECKPOINT 26

Note the recurring mockingbird **motif**. Why could Jem also be linked to the mockingbird theme here?

GLOSSARY

The Grey Ghost a book referred to right at the start of the novel; this could be used to achieve a sense of a completed circle and to remind us how the children felt about the ghost of Boo at the beginning

EXAMINER'S SECRET

The repetition of themes often gives an indicator of a message the writer is trying to portray. The end of the text is also a good place to look for a summary of the writer's point of view.

in the same way that Atticus has done in the previous trial of Tom Robinson (see **Theme** on **Structure**).

As Scout is looking back on events, summarising the story in a dream-like fashion, she refers to herself and Jem as 'his children' and 'Boo's children' (Ch. 31, pp. 307–8). This has religious overtones of 'God's children' and therefore implies that Boo has been watching over Scout and Jem through the episodes of the novel.

Everything has now been concluded: Scout has seen Boo, Robert Ewell is dead and justice has been achieved. Likewise the **genre** of **bildungsroman** (see **Theme** on **Growing up**) has been satisfied, as Scout considers 'there wasn't much left for us to learn' (Ch. 31, p. 308), now truly understanding Atticus's maxim and therefore holding no fear. However, Scout still has a few years to go until she is able to look back as a more mature narrator.

CHECKPOINT 27

Has the reader been prepared by earlier incidents for Boo to save the children?

Now take a break!

WHO SAYS ...?

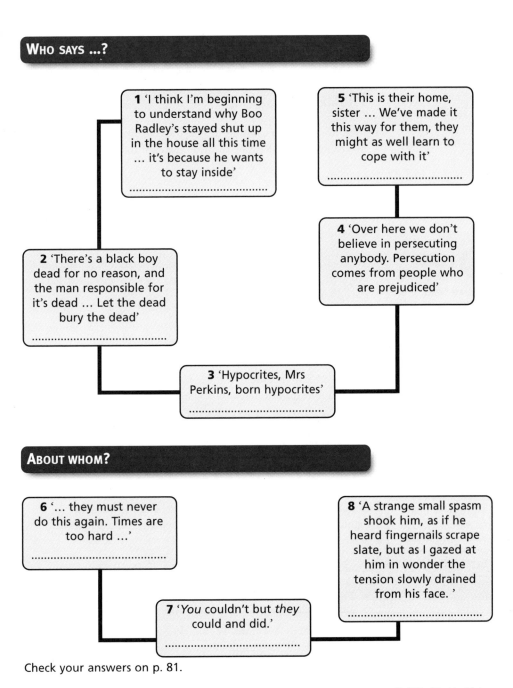

1 'I think I'm beginning to understand why Boo Radley's stayed shut up in the house all this time ... it's because he wants to stay inside'

....

5 'This is their home, sister ... We've made it this way for them, they might as well learn to cope with it'

....

4 'Over here we don't believe in persecuting anybody. Persecution comes from people who are prejudiced'

....

2 'There's a black boy dead for no reason, and the man responsible for it's dead ... Let the dead bury the dead'

....

3 'Hypocrites, Mrs Perkins, born hypocrites'

....

ABOUT WHOM?

6 '... they must never do this again. Times are too hard ...'

....

8 'A strange small spasm shook him, as if he heard fingernails scrape slate, but as I gazed at him in wonder the tension slowly drained from his face. '

....

7 '*You* couldn't but *they* could and did.'

....

Check your answers on p. 81.

PART THREE

COMMENTARY

THEMES

Structure, characters, setting, language and imagery all play a part in advancing and emphasising the key themes of the novel. These are:

- Growing up
- Courage
- Prejudice
- Symbolism

CHECK THE BOOK

Mildred Taylor's *Roll of Thunder, Hear My Cry* (1976) has many of the same themes. It is told by a black girl narrator and set in 1930s southern America. Compare and contrast.

The minor themes of Family, Loneliness, Superstition, Injustice and Hypocrisy fall within the Commentary. (They are also discussed in **Part Two** of these Notes.)

GROWING UP

To Kill a Mockingbird is about the narrator's growth of awareness. In these Notes, Chapters 1–11 are referred to as 'Lessons the Children Learn' because these chapters focus specifically on Scout and Jem. But the learning does not stop here and a new lesson is learned about some aspect of life in almost every chapter, for instance through their observation of, and participation in, events during and following the trial.

Scout

CHECKPOINT 28

Try to remember an example of when the reader understands events better than Scout.

The story is told by a mature narrator who is looking back on herself as a child. Scout's naivety and childish view of the world is highlighted by the reader often understanding events better than Scout herself.

Over the course of the novel Scout learns various lessons:

- From Calpurnia: that politeness should be shown to all people even if their manners differ from your own (Chapter 3)
- From Atticus: to control her impetuosity (Chapter 9) and to appreciate the various meanings of courage (Chapters 10 and 11), to learn tolerance and to be able to turn the other cheek

- From Aunt Alexandra: the value of being a lady (Chapter 24)
- From Heck Tate and Atticus: the destructive implications of society's prejudice, even if Scout has not yet been able to fully appreciate why prejudice exists (Trial chapters, Aftermath and closing chapters)

Scout's important educational experiences all seem to take place outside school. She is switched off by school where the teachers' lessons seem to be totally out of context to the children's lives.

By the end of the novel Scout has successfully managed to take on Atticus's key lesson in the novel – that of seeing another person's point of view. Her behaviour with Boo has transformed dramatically from that at the beginning. However she is still a child, and after her traumatic incident with Robert Ewell she comes back to her reading of *The Grey Ghost*, a book that she was reading at the beginning of the novel. She feels she has learned all she can for the moment.

Jem

Jem's growing up is much quicker and more radical. While we observe Scout maturing, she comments on her brother's growth. This growth is easier to chart because:

- Jem is one of the closest people to the narrator.
- It is easier to report more about another character (i.e. Jem) than what is happening to oneself (Scout).

At the beginning of the novel Jem likes to play superstitious games about Boo Radley with Scout and Dill. The start of Jem's period of maturing is marked when:

- Jem goes to get his trousers (Chapter 6) and Scout comments 'Jem and I first began to part company' (p. 63).
- Jem organises the building of the snowman. He does not see this as a game, but takes a mature attitude to finding the resources which are needed (Chapter 8).
- Jem begins to recognise Boo's human side (Chapter 9) and the childish games discontinue.

CHECK THE BOOK

Charles Dickens' *Hard Times* (1854) similarly depicts an education system irrelevant to the children's everyday existence.

In contrast, Scout does not really appreciate the true nature of Boo's personality until the end of the novel. She is a few steps behind Jem in this process of growing up.

CHECKPOINT 29

Find an example of Scout and Dill's naivety, which highlights the gap of maturity between them and Jem.

Jem gradually becomes more separate from Scout and Dill, particularly after his punishment involving Mrs Dubose (Chapter 11), after which time Scout notices he is acquiring 'an alien set of values' (Ch. 12, p. 127). Instead of encouraging Scout's tomboy character, he tells her she should be more respectful of his aunt and start 'bein' a girl and acting right' (Ch. 12, p. 127). He breaks 'the remaining code of our childhood' (Ch. 14, p. 155) when he goes to tell Atticus that Dill is in the house, having run away. Jem is proud about showing Scout his first signs of physical maturity (Ch. 23, p. 249) and suffers teenage angst in his response to the injustices of the trial (Chapters 22–3). Although not a child anymore, he is having trouble coming to terms with the adult world. We are constantly reminded of this uncertain transition when he acts responsibly and with maturity at times, but he has a child's understanding in many other respects, for instance when he misinterprets the mob of men outside their house as meaning trouble (Chapter 15).

EXAMINER'S SECRET

See how points about Jem growing up are backed up with specfic examples and short quotations. Make sure you do this in your essays yourself.

By the end of the novel Jem has taken on some adult attitudes and views. He has learned from Atticus's example, for instance when he tries to make Scout feel better about her mistake after the pageant (Chapter 28). Jem's movement from childhood to adulthood is acknowledged in different ways by the adults in his life: Miss Maudie gives him a slice from the cake (Chapter 22) and Calpurnia has anticipated this change earlier by the respectful title of 'Mister Jem' (Ch. 12, p. 127).

COURAGE

CHECKPOINT 30

Consider whether Aunt Alexandra coming to live with the Finches at a difficult time is a good example of a courageous act.

There are many examples of courage shown throughout the novel. For instance:

- Chuck Little stands up to Burris Ewell in class (Chapter 3).
- Jem rescues his trousers at night from the Radley Place (Chapter 6).
- Miss Maudie is optimistic after her house has burned down (Chapter 8).

- Mr Link Deas speaks out for the Robinsons (Chapters 19 and 27).

Two major types of courage are emphasised in the novel:

- 'Real courage' (Ch. 11, p. 124) – when you continue with what you are doing even though you are fighting a losing battle. An example is Mrs Dubose's battle with her morphine addiction
- Fighting against evil and prejudice. Understanding of others is sometimes not enough; an act of bravery is demanded to try to prevent evil taking place and to override prejudice. Examples of this type of courage are:
  - Mr Underwood's article about Tom Robinson's death (Chapter 25)
  - Boo Radley's heroic act when he rescues Jem from Robert Ewell (Chapter 28)

Both these main types of courage are evident in the major plot of the novel:

- Atticus represents Tom Robinson even though success is unlikely.
- He makes a stand against racial prejudice in the Maycomb community (see **Theme** on **Prejudice**).

PREJUDICE

Prejudice is arguably the most prominent theme of the novel. It is directed towards groups and individuals in the Maycomb community. Prejudice is linked with ideas of fear, superstition and injustice.

Groups

Race

Racial prejudice consumes the mob (Chapter 15) which wishes to prevent Tom Robinson even gaining a court hearing (the basic form of justice). It is the fiercest form of prejudice in the novel.

- The abolition of slavery (such as Calpurnia's ancestors) after the American Civil War of 1861–5 changed the legal position of black people in American society.

> **CHECKPOINT 31**
>
> As you think about this theme, consider whether *To Kill a Mockingbird* is a courageous novel.

- This freedom initially made life much harder for the black community and black and white people remained segregated in all aspects of life until the second half of the twentieth century (see **Author and context**). White people now saw black people as potential competitors for jobs, particularly in the hard years of the Economic Depression during which *To Kill a Mockingbird* is set.
- Fear and paranoia led to the 'white' belief that black people desired all that white people had, including their women.

EXAMINER'S SECRET

Keep a list of examples under headings for the main themes. This will be useful for writing essays and revision.

As you are reading consider other examples of racial prejudice (apart from the case of Tom Robinson). For example:

- Aunt Alexandra's attitude to Calpurnia
- The Missionary tea ladies' comments about black people
- The segregation in Maycomb
- People's views of Dolphus Raymond, a white man living with a black woman

Class and family groups

Maycomb is divided into clearly defined groups which characterise position and status in society. Jem recognises the class structure when he tells Scout in Chapter 23 that there are 'four kinds of folks in the world' (Ch. 23, p. 249). These are:

- The Finches and their neighbours (the white middle class)
- The Cunninghams (who represent the badly hit farming community)
- The Ewells (the lowest class of white people)
- The black community (automatically seen as at the bottom of the social strata)

The Ewells, universally despised by the Maycomb community as 'White Trash' (the term commonly used to refer to the lowest social group of white people, typically very poor, uneducated, dirty and crude) would most keenly feel the threat of black people. Due to the abolition of slavery there was no longer a clear distinction of boundaries between the white lower-class and the black community.

When Tom shows that he felt sorry for Mayella (a crime worse than rape in the white jury's eyes) this would be seen as the lowest class of citizen showing superiority towards a class above (and a white woman – see discussion of **Gender** below). The white community's fear of racial disturbance and their insecurity about their own position in society meant that Tom Robinson was found guilty. This maintained the traditional hierarchies in the community, at least for the time being (i.e. until the Black Civil Rights Movement of the late 1950s/early 1960s).

Aunt Alexandra is obsessed with heredity and educating Scout and Jem about their superior family background. She will not allow Scout to bring a Cunningham, from a poor, conservative but proud and decent farming family, home to play, nor allow Scout to visit Calpurnia at her home. Every family group in Maycomb, according to Aunt Alexandra, had a particular 'Streak' (Ch. 13, p. 143 and Ch. 23, p. 247). Scout documents the 'caste system' (Ch. 13, p. 145), where, due to the inward growing and isolated nature of the community, distinct and very particular family characteristics have developed (Ch. 13, p. 145). We see how beneath the restrictions of the class system there is further categorising of people in their presumptions about family groups, rather than seeing each person as an individual.

Gender

Local history in the novel tells us that the females at Finch's Landing were kept on a tight reign, just like the slaves (Chapter 9). At the time the novel is set, women were still regarded as unequal to men. Scout learns about women's position from:

- Miss Maudie in terms of religion (Chapter 5)
- Atticus in terms of the law – they were not permitted to sit on the jury (Chapter 23)
- Aunt Alexandra in terms of expected behaviour and dress (throughout the novel)

However, an idealised view of women was held at the time of the novel. The Southern Gentleman was expected to show chivalry and protection to Southern Belles and the idea of Southern Womanhood was that women were to be worshipped and protected.

 DID YOU KNOW?

Class prejudice is closely tied up with racial prejudice.

CHECKPOINT 32

Mayella knew this well when she played on the white men's conscience at the trial. How did she do this?

Tom Robinson in terms of race, class and gender

We see therefore that by the time Tom Robinson had his hearing it was more complicated than racial prejudice. To some extent, class and gender prejudice also contributed to the unjust verdict of guilty.

Individuals

Prejudice is directed towards individual characters in the novel who do not fit into the expected behavioural patterns of society and about whom little is known. These prejudices are fed by:

- Fear – for example, the children are frightened of Boo Radley, an outsider to society whom they have never seen.
- Rumour – Jem, Scout and Dill have heard rumours about Boo, from Miss Stephanie and other children at school.
- Superstition – superstitious views of ghosts, and stories they have learned from growing up in the Maycomb community, feed into their fear of Boo Radley.

CHECKPOINT 33

Think of further examples of prejudice shown towards individuals and consider if these examples are linked to group prejudice.

When the children's experience of the world increases and they realise that Boo is a real person, capable of suffering like everyone else, prejudice towards him dies.

Other individuals who are targets for prejudice are:

- Miss Maudie, by the foot-washers, for her love of nature and unconventional religious views
- Atticus for his defence of a black man
- Tom Robinson himself

Harper Lee seems to indicate that the breaking down of prejudice has to be targeted towards individuals initially, for instance like the Cunningham man at the trial. A 'baby-step' (Miss Maudie, Ch. 22, p. 238) has to be taken instead of solving prejudice all at once.

Solutions to prejudice

The author seems to be presenting two solutions to getting rid of prejudice:

- Atticus's maxim
- Harper Lee's challenge of stereotypes

Atticus's maxim

(could also be referred to as a motif of sympathy)

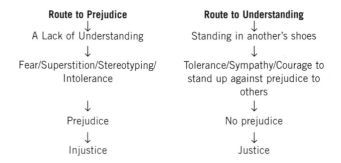

Route to Prejudice	Route to Understanding
↓	↓
A Lack of Understanding	Standing in another's shoes
↓	↓
Fear/Superstition/Stereotyping/ Intolerance	Tolerance/Sympathy/Courage to stand up against prejudice to others
↓	↓
Prejudice	No prejudice
↓	↓
Injustice	Justice

Atticus's **maxim** follows that if you attempt to stand in another's shoes or another's skin you will be able to see their point of view and there will be an understanding and tolerance and therefore no prejudice. This is repeated to the children and demonstrated by Atticus, for instance when he tries to sympathise with Mrs Dubose and Robert Ewell. We see that Scout and Jem, as time goes by, learn to do this with various characters, for instance Mayella Ewell and Boo Radley (see **Theme** on **Growing up**).

It is shown to be a very effective maxim which can be applied to almost anybody. Atticus tries to get others to do this (for instance the white people in the trial to stand in Tom Robinson's shoes) and he attempts to do it himself. He even tries to get into the dirty skin of Robert Ewell, although this finally defeats him. Even Atticus has reached his bottom line of tolerance (a sign of his humanity?). We are left with an unresolved question – what to do about extreme characters who seem untouchable by reason and are inherently evil? Harper Lee does not seem to be able to provide an answer to this question here.

> **CHECKPOINT 34**
>
> Try to find as many examples as possible where Atticus's maxim is stated.

Harper Lee's challenge of stereotypes

People often stereotype others out of ignorance. Harper Lee seems to be challenging the traditional stereotypes in American fiction by her sensitive portrayal of particular characters in *To Kill a Mockingbird*.

The Negroes

Black people were viewed as either evil human beings or stupid, lovable and childlike creatures. Harper Lee makes her black characters, Calpurnia and Tom Robinson, normal human beings capable of the same thoughts and feelings as white people. She shows the reader that although they are considered of lower class than people like the Ewells, they are more law-abiding, more hard working, more house-proud.

The Southern Gentleman

As indicated above, the Southern Gentleman would have been traditionally represented as a gallant and extremely courteous gentleman, who worshipped the idea of Southern Womanhood above all else. Through Atticus, Harper Lee challenges this stereotype. He is polite to everyone in an equal sort of way, and we remember him saying to Aunt Alexandra that he is 'in favour of Southern womanhood as much as anybody, but not for preserving polite fiction at the expense of human life' (Ch. 15, p. 162).

The Southern Belle and Southern Womanhood

The idea of ladylike behaviour and feminine dress was accepted and expected of young girls like Scout who should be brought up to be Southern Belles. Harper Lee shows that Scout does not fit into this mould and that her clothes are mocked (see **Theme** on **Symbolism**) by Aunt Alexandra's missionary circle friends (Chapter 24). Unlike Aunt Alexandra, Atticus is not concerned with making Scout into 'a ray of sunshine' (Ch. 9, p. 90), but Harper Lee does go some way into accepting the idealised stereotype when she eventually makes Scout sympathetic to being a lady.

Harper Lee's aim for readers of *To Kill a Mockingbird* seems to be to live the lives of her characters, to live Atticus's maxim, and by doing this to make them appreciate similar unknown characters in their own communities – especially the black community whom, at that time, many white people would have known little about. Above all, her message is that it is 'a sin' to harm an innocent (see **Theme** on **Symbolism**). Harper Lee does not imply that there is a quick and easy process to the solving of prejudice, which is one of the reasons why *To Kill a Mockingbird* is such a realistic novel.

SYMBOLISM

The mockingbird motif

The mockingbird is the most significant **symbol** in the novel. This repeated image and its key symbol of an innocent creature make it a strong **motif**. A mockingbird is a type of finch, a small, plain bird with beautiful song which 'mocks' or mimics other birds' song. There are different species of the bird, some of which are endangered, and it is thought that their habits differ according to their adaption to specific environments.

The mockingbird first appears in Chapter 10 of *To Kill a Mockingbird* when Atticus is telling the children how to use their shotguns: 'Shoot all the bluejays you want, if you can hit 'em, but remember it's a sin to kill a mockingird' (Ch. 10, p. 99). Scout is surprised to hear the nonjudgemental Atticus calling anything a 'sin'. Miss Maudie explains to her that this is because mockingbirds are neither harmful nor destructive, and only make nice music for people to enjoy.

The symbol for Boo Radley and Tom Robinson is not drawn together until Scout's comment at the end when she recognises that the public exposure of Boo Radley would be 'sort of like shootin' a mockingbird' (Ch. 30, p. 304). However, although not made explicit previously, it is evident that both characters have mockingbird traits:

- They both show kindness – Boo to the children, Tom to Mayella.
- They are both innocent – Boo of the evil persona with which he is associated and Tom of the crime of rape.
- Both are victims of prejudice (see **Theme** on **Prejudice**).
- Both are imprisoned and potentially vulnerable – Boo is imprisoned in a separate world to protect him from people's prejudice if exposed, as Heck Tate, Atticus and Scout recognise at

CHECK THE NET

To find out more about the nature of the mockingbird and its song, and to see some pictures go to the following websites:

www.lsjunction .com/mock.html
www.birdsforever. com/mock.html
www.holoweb. com/cannon/ northngn. htm

CHECK THE BOOK

The mockingbird is not a completely new symbol and appears in other places in American literature and folklore, e.g. Walt Whitman's *Out of the Cradle Endlessly Rocking*.

the end of the novel. Tom is imprisoned and later killed as a result of people's prejudice.

Atticus, a mockingbird too in a sense, has sung Tom's song of truth to the people of Maycomb but has not been heard.

The mockingbird symbol is kept alive for the reader throughout the narrative, therefore continually reminding us of the themes with which it is associated. For instance, it is referred to:

- After the mad dog incident (Ch. 10, p. 105)
- When waiting for the jury's verdict (Ch. 21, p. 232)
- In Mr Underwood's article about Tom's death (Ch. 25, p. 265)
- When Scout and Jem are on their way to the pageant (Ch. 28, p. 281)

At tense moments, like on the way to the pageant, even the mockingbird is silent. In moments of descriptive beauty the mockingbird is often alluded to, lurking somewhere in the background.

Harper Lee invites the reader to consider the word 'mockingbird' and all its associations:

- The children mock Boo's life as they make fun of and imitate it.
- Mayella accuses Atticus of mocking her.
- The trial is a mockery of justice.

Other symbols

The significance of the mockingbird motif therefore broadens out to contain many layers of meaning. The mockingbird is not the only symbol in the novel. Other examples of the author using a description to allude to something else are:

- The Radley house, with its closed doors and shutters and austere front, represents the privacy, isolation and unfriendliness of the Radley family.
- The tree beside the Radley Place represents Boo's character and his desire to communicate, when presents are left in the tree.

When the hole is closed up (Chapter 7) Boo's contact is being denied, but when the children stand near the tree watching the fire (Chapter 8) contact is established again. Much later (Chapter 26) Scout notices the tree trunk swelling and soon afterwards Boo saves the children and Bob Ewell is found dead under the tree (Chapter 28).

- Scout and Jem's snowman represents how superficial skin colour is to the essence of a human being. There is not much snow and there is a lot of mud, so the snowman is dark until Jem covers it with bits of snow he has found. It keeps changing colour and during the fire the snowman collapses altogether.

- Mrs Dubose's camellias represent the prejudices which cannot be brushed off easily. They have to be tugged by their roots.

STRUCTURE

NARRATIVE STRUCTURE

The story of the novel follows the lives of the Finch family between 1933 and 1935. The string of events between these dates is **chronologically** arranged. It starts when Scout is explaining the period on which she is looking back. By the end of the novel, the story has come a full circle.

The novel divides into two parts:

- Part 1 (Chapters 1–11) focuses on the children's games, with Boo Radley as the driving force.

- Part 2 (Chapters 12–31) is centred on the 'adult's game' of Tom Robinson's trial.

In Part 1 of the novel the children learn information that the reader needs to know for Part 2. The children's prejudices in Part 1 are reflected with much more destructive implications by the adults in Part 2. For the purpose of these York Notes the novel has been broken into three sections in the Detailed Summaries section, 'Lessons the Children Learn', 'Trial Times' and 'Aftermath'. The 'Aftermath' (Chapters 22–31) comes after both the children's and

EXAMINER'S SECRET
By reading the novel several more times symbols will be discovered that have not been noticed before. Discussion of more obscure symbols you find will show that you have looked at the text thoroughly and thought carefully about the possible meanings the writer is trying to put across.

CHECKPOINT 36
Why did the novel not end after the trial scene (Chapter 21) or Tom's death (Chapters 24–5)?

adults' games and draws these two plots together when Boo Radley rescues the children from Robert Ewell, who is seeking revenge after the Tom Robinson trial. Harper Lee's **epigraph** clearly flags the two important elements in the novel – 'lawyers' and 'children'.

INTERNAL STRUCTURE

CHECKPOINT 37

A critic has argued that the two plots are too different to be linked convincingly. Do you agree? Another view is that they are not meant to be linked as they are there for a contrast.

One chapter of the novel cannot be viewed in isolation from another, as the events within the story have been arranged to develop ideas within the text. Repetitions and echoes, and the way in which chapters balance each other, make the major themes much sharper. For example, the juxtaposition of the shooting of the mad dog (Chapter 10) and Mrs Dubose's death from a morphine overdose (Chapter 11) presents strongly contrasting ideas about the theme of courage.

Another technique that Harper Lee uses is to present the reader with background information about a character, a group of characters or a situation. This works in two ways:

- It offers the reader an insight into a particular way of life.
- It subsequently becomes of significance in a different context.

We also see evidence of careful structuring in an individual character's speech. Atticus, for instance, asks Mayella about her family background before he questions her about the alleged rape. He asks Tom about his previous crime conviction before he asks him about the situation with Mayella. He plans his order of questions as he knows that this will have a particular effect on the jury listening.

Equally, Harper Lee knows that this order will keep the reader's interest. We discover about Tom's hand early on in the trial scene, but it is only later that we realise the significance of this apparently irrelevant piece of information. The craft that has gone into making this novel a work of art can only be fully appreciated when the whole story has been told. The secret lies in careful planning, particularly with a long novel like *To Kill a Mockingbird*.

The next time that you are telling someone about an incident, stop and consider why you are giving them some information before or next to other information and how you are using particular language (see section on Language and style for more information on internal structure). You will see that structure is an integral and natural part of every type of narrative.

CHARACTERS

This is one view of who the most important characters are in the novel. You may disagree! List your main characters.

ATTICUS

Atticus is a single parent and nearly fifty years old when we meet him. We learn of his approach to bringing up his children when Scout says, 'he played with us, read to us, and treated us with courteous detachment' (Ch. 1 p. 6). His sister, Aunt Alexandra, does not approve of his parenting, particularly with Scout who is far too masculine for her liking. Atticus believes in being honest and straightforward with Jem and Scout, always listening to their opinion and answering difficult questions, even the embarrassing ones. He treats them with respect, for example allowing them to come back to hear the trial verdict, even though he must realise there may be implications later. Scout and Jem learn to respect him for being a constant, principled and sympathetic figure. Such a style as Atticus's may have seemed very modern at the time.

Father of Jem and Scout

Maycomb's lawyer and conscience

Fair-minded

Courteous

Miss Maudie comments on his consistency of character, whether privately at home or publicly in town. His conduct is always gentlemanly (see discussion of Southern Gentleman in **Theme** on **Prejudice**) despite provocation.

Courageous

Teacher of life's morals

Atticus's self-respect and pride demand that he makes sure Tom Robinson gets a fair trial. His case is ordered and his oratory is admired (see **Language and Structure**). His views are enlightened and he is a man of extreme courage, fighting against the prejudice of his community (see **Themes** on **Courage** and **Prejudice**).

 CHECK THE FILM

Do you think Gregory Peck was a good choice of actor to play Atticus in the film version of the novel?

He has some weaknesses (see Chapters 15 and 23–7), though these are the weaknesses of the idealist. We may feel that he takes undue risk with the lives of both himself and his children.

DID YOU KNOW?

In ancient times Atticus was a philosopher, well-known for his kindly character and for his love of truth.

Atticus could be considered to be the main character in the novel. He embodies the themes of justice, tolerance, goodness and courage. He is a man of extreme integrity, and it is through his mouth that Harper Lee expresses her moral philosophy.

See Atticus's maxim (see **Theme** on **Prejudice**) for the way he aims to understand people as if he were inside them.

SCOUT

Scout competes with Atticus for main character status. Events are seen through her eyes. She is nearly six at the beginning, and the narrative is about the next three years of her life. We see a big change in her (see **Theme** on **Growing up**). However, throughout the novel her character is strengthened, rather than altered, by her experiences.

Narrator
Age: almost six to almost nine
Tomboy
Bright, observant
Confident, friendly
Innocent
Nonjudgemental

Through her confident and sociable nature the reader meets a variety of different characters and encounters a range of situations. (This is an essential characteristic for the mature narrator to be able to tell her story.) She does not always understand everything, she is not judgemental, but she demonstrates an ability to absorb what is going on.

Scout is intelligent but she is also fun and, as a tomboy, happiest in her overalls. This is understandable when her main role models are male. (Her mother died when she was two.) She gives her elder brother 'hero' status, and has a loving relationship with her father who is often seen as god-like. The women she is closest to are Cal, who helps to look after her, and unconventional Miss Maudie. Despite making an effort to be more ladylike as time goes by, we wonder if Scout will ever be other than different. (See **Theme** on **Prejudice**.)

The mature Scout

The mature narrator remains unknown to us. She is telling the story of her experience as a child. She is only a mouthpiece, stepping back into her childhood skin (see **Atticus's maxim**). But we do discover, by telling such a story, that the grown-up Scout is intelligent, creative and informative about history, literature and Southern ways (like Harper Lee?).

JEM

Jem is a few years older than Scout and as a constant companion he participates in most of the events that are described.

In general he is rational and intelligent. On the occasion when he isn't, and cuts off Mrs Dubose's camellias, he learns his biggest lesson on courage. However, Jem is going through a time of physical and mental change, so atypical behaviour is in keeping with this. (See **Theme** on **Growing up** for more on Jem and his transition from childhood to adulthood.)

Jem is a natural leader. His creative and resourceful nature is brought out in the games he plays with Dill and Scout. Jem is a mirror of Atticus, even in his ambition to become a lawyer to effect change. Scout notices the similarity when she comments, 'Jem was becoming almost as good as Atticus at making you feel right when things went wrong' (Ch. 28, p. 285). The novelist seems to imply that what has not been achieved by Atticus may later be achieved by Jem – reassuring us that there will be people like Atticus in the future.

Scout's brother
Nearly ten to almost thirteen
Courageous
Resourceful
Idealistic, thoughtful
Strong sense of justice

CALPURNIA (CAL)

Calpurnia is the Finch family cook, but she also plays a big part in bringing up Scout and Jem. She has gained Atticus's respect and acknowledgement as a 'faithful member of the family' (Ch. 14, p. 150). She is strict with the children, but also has a sense of compassion and is kind to them when they are finding life difficult.

Cal takes Scout and Jem to the black community church, fussing over their appearance as if they were her own children. Scout is surprised to find that Cal has another life: an extended family, she speaks a different language and has alternative ways of doing things. Scout also learns that Cal's origins were at Finch's Landing and how she learned to read out of a book that Scout's grandfather gave her. There is a certain **irony** in this, as it is from Cal that Scout has learned to write.

Cal represents the bridge between the white and black communities. She gives Atticus information about the Robinson family; Atticus uses her to thank the black community for their gifts to him, but

Finch family cook
Surrogate mother
Firm yet kind
Bridge with black community
Ex-slave stock

reminds Cal to tell them that they mustn't do this again as life is hard. Cal is the person that Atticus chooses to accompany him to tell Helen Robinson of her husband's death.

DILL (CHARLES BAKER HARRIS)

Dill comes from Mississippi every summer to stay with his Aunt Rachel and to play with Jem and Scout. He features largely in the first eleven chapters of the novel where he is fascinated with Boo Radley and goads Jem and Scout into trying to see this mystery figure. Through these incidents we learn of his curious and quick-thinking nature.

In the second part of the novel Dill is only present as a contrast to Jem and Scout – we do not see this character mature as we do with the others. At the trial Dill's sensitive nature is contrasted with the logical and rational Scout. Whereas Jem wants to confront prejudice, Dill decides to accept things the way they are and make the best of them – consequently his choice of profession will be a laughing clown! Dill provides for Scout a practical example in family dynamics. He feels unwanted by his fractured family but she knows only love from her single parent. Dill dwells in his 'own twilight world' (Ch. 14, p. 158); perhaps his wild imagination is stimulated by an unhappiness in his everyday existence.

From Mississippi
Age: nearly seven
to nearly ten
Curious
Vivid imagination
Sensitive
Unstable family

AUNT ALEXANDRA

Alexandra Finch is Jem and Scout's aunt. She lives at Finch's Landing which is associated with a past of cotton-growing and slave-owning. Unlike her brothers, she has not moved away and made a new life for herself and perhaps consequently, as Scout discovers, she holds onto traditional views and is obsessed with family heredity.

She first features in the story when Atticus, Jem and Scout go to spend Christmas at Finch's Landing. She disapproves of Scout's tomboy ways. She becomes a major character in the plot when she invites herself to stay at the Finch home in Maycomb, to help Atticus with the children during the difficult trial period. The Finch family seemed to get better with Calpurnia and without Aunt Alexandra! Aunt Alexandra and Atticus have fundamentally different attitudes to child rearing and servant supervision.

Although Aunt Alexandra is not favourably portrayed by Scout, she has several redeeming moments – most notably when she detaches herself from the hypocritical Missionary Society meeting and expresses emotional sympathy for Atticus at the news of Tom's death. She picks up her dignity and returns to her guests, and Scout, all at once, appreciates this lady's behaviour.

> Sister of Atticus and Jack
> Family-oriented
> Proud
> Racist
> Traditional, rigid
> Sympathetic?

MISS MAUDIE ATKINSON

As Scout and Jem's neighbour, who is always out working in her garden, Miss Maudie is a source of information and company for the children. As with Calpurnia, the reader feels positive towards this character as a result of Scout and Atticus liking and valuing her. She does not talk down to them but gives them respect, although they do not always understand her. She talks to Scout about the problems of rigid religion, of what Arthur Radley was like as a child, of Atticus's talents. She disapproves of neighbourhood gossip and prejudice. She dislikes how the town comes out to watch 'a poor devil on trial for his life' (Ch. 16, p. 176), and silences Mrs Merriweather over her hypocrisy at Aunt Alexandra's tea-party.

> Down-to-earth
> Sharp-witted
> Supporter of Atticus
> Mother figure

Her major role in the plot therefore seems to be to reinforce Atticus's philosophy, and to be a constant, reassuring and sensible model for the children when Atticus is busy elsewhere.

MRS HENRY LAFAYETTE DUBOSE

Mrs Dubose is known in the neighbourhood as the 'meanest old woman who ever lived' (Ch. 4, p. 39). In contrast to Miss Maudie who represents the friendly side of the community, Mrs Dubose represents the traditional and prejudiced side. Jem and Scout try to avoid her as Atticus has told them that they must maintain politeness even though her language is 'vicious' (Ch. 11, p. 110).

> Another Finch neighbour
> Old and ill
> Typical Maycomb values
> Cantankerous, racist
> Lonely?
> Courageous?

It is Mrs Dubose's shouting of racist comments to the children about Atticus, that makes Jem finally lose his temper and behead her camellias. She chooses to punish him by making him read to her every night for a month. This punishment is indicative of somebody who is desperately lonely and seems to need distracting. When she dies the children learn that she was struggling to combat a morphine addiction. Atticus uses this to teach them a lesson on courage. Mrs Dubose is initially a very flat character but a complex personality emerges. As a character she surfaces and disappears within one chapter.

HECK TATE

Town sheriff
Trial witness
Upholder of justice
Intuitive
Respectful
Realistic

Heck Tate is the Maycomb sheriff, a friend of Atticus's, who appears at three significant moments in the novel:

- when the mad dog is shot

- to warn Atticus of imminent trouble when Tom is moved to the local gaol

- as a key witness at the trial

However, it is not until the final chapters of the novel that the reader really gets to know the character. Although he is an 'official' person like Atticus, he realises the limitations of the legal system, and persuades Atticus to let justice be. He shows great insight and respect for another human being when he suggests to Atticus that Boo Radley's act was heroic but should be kept quiet.

TOM ROBINSON

Honest
Kind
Polite
Mockingbird?

Tom Robinson, like Boo Radley, is a minor character who is not explored in great depth. However he is crucial in developing the overall themes and symbols of the novel.

Tom is married to Helen and they have three children. The family is part of the respectable, church-going black community. Tom is revealed as polite and honourable in court, where he was shown to be happy to help Mayella for no payment. His perception of her loneliness and need, however, gets him into trouble. Atticus proves his innocence, physically visible by his crippled left arm. However, as a **symbol** of the black community (see **Theme** on **Prejudice**) Tom is found guilty. In despair, he tries to escape from gaol and is shot 'in cold blood'.

BOO (ARTHUR) RADLEY

Boo Radley is a largely mysterious figure, whose childhood misdemeanours have led to a lifetime's imprisonment. As well as by the wider community, he is mocked by Jem, Scout and Dill and is the focus for their childhood games. His character gradually emerges. He leaves gifts for the children. He wraps a blanket around Scout's shoulders during the fire. He is a lonely, kind figure, benignly watching over Scout and Jem's lives.

Feared, unknown
Imprisoned
Lonely
Kind
Heroic
Mockingbird?

It is not until the end of the novel that he is 'seen' by Scout, both physically and metaphorically, when he heroically rescues Jem from Robert Ewell.

THE EWELLS

Robert Ewell, father of the family, represents the 'White Trash' element of the community. He has no job and spends his relief cheques on whisky, leaving the oldest of his many children to try and look after the family. We know from our encounter with Burris Ewell in the early chapters that this is an impossible task.

At the trial Robert Ewell is rude, bigoted and foul-mouthed (see **Language and style**). There is a strong indication that it was he who beat up Mayella. His vicious act of revenge against Tom, Atticus and Judge Taylor forms the driving force of the final chapters.

He shoots game on other people's land. His children are quite out of control (*truance par excellence*), and he cannot even keep the job he gets when he attempts respectability. In dying at the end, the novelist seems to be saying that he is beyond hope and/or that justice must seen to be done.

Poor
Racist
Unreliable
Foul-mouthed
Ill-educated
Hopeless?

However, there is some unlikely opportunity for optimism in his daughter Mayella. Scout recognises that it is love, support and company that Mayella lacks. This lack of love, warmth and human contact leads Mayella to grab Tom. She wants to be kissed by a man: what happens with her father (an incestuous relationship is hinted at) 'don't count' (Ch. 14, p. 214). She is a pathetic figure at the trial, who does not seem to be able, for fear of her father, to tell the truth. Perhaps, by Robert Ewell's death there is hope for the future, as the fear that was the barrier to truth and understanding has been removed. Mayella's flowers at the Ewell residence can now begin to flourish.

THE CUNNINGHAMS

Poor

Racist, mob leaders

Proud

People of the land

Thoughtful

Hope for the future?

The Cunninghams resemble the Ewells, but only initially. They are dignified, proud people, as is shown by Walter not wishing to accept his teacher's money. His father also shows this by paying Atticus for his law work in ways other than money. Mr Cunningham shows a basic goodness in dispersing the racist mob when his eyes are opened by Scout. A different member of the family, one of the jurors, has great difficulty finding Tom guilty. Harper Lee is showing that there is potential for the future if there are groups of people like these, as they have temporarily stood in another's shoes and seen their viewpoint. (See **Themes** on **Courage** and **Prejudice**.)

MINOR CHARACTERS

In order of appearance in the novel:

Simon Finch – ancestor of Scout's, who established Finch's Landing in Alabama and owned a cotton farm on which slaves worked

Uncle Jack – Atticus and Aunt Alexandra's younger brother, a doctor who lives in Nashville. He returns to Maycomb every Christmas, and Scout and Jem know him as the fun and friendly bachelor-uncle, who teaches them to shoot and flirts with Miss Maudie. He is close to Atticus in his open-minded views

Miss Rachel Haverford – a Finch neighbour, aunt of Dill

Mr and Mrs Radley and Nathan – parents and older brother of Boo, rarely seen outside their house; Boo's keepers/protectors

Miss Stephanie Crawford – a Finch neighbour, with a light-hearted nature and concerned with triviality and local gossip

Miss Caroline Fisher and Miss Gates – Scout's schoolteachers

Doctor Reynolds – Maycomb doctor and family friend

Little Chuck Little – a member of Scout's class; of poor background and a 'born gentleman'

Cecil Jacobs – Scout's classmate and neighbour; taunts Scout with prejudice of her father; jumps out on Jem and Scout on their way to the pageant

Mr Avery – superstitious Finch neighbour

Eula May – Maycomb's telephone operator

Judge John Taylor – the elderly judge in the Tom Robinson trial; of high moral calibre and unconventional behaviour

Cousin Ike Finch – Finch relative; a confederate veteran, who still lives the American Civil War in his mind

Uncle Jimmy – Aunt Alexandra's husband; a quiet man

Francis – Alexandra and Jimmy's grandson

Zeebo – Calpurnia's son; reads hymns at the black community church; the local garbage collector

Jesse – black lady who looks after Mrs Dubose

Lula May – black lady who objects to Scout and Jem being at the black community church

Reverend Sykes – leader of the black community church; he finds seats for Jem, Scout and Dill at the trial and offers his viewpoint of events

Helen Robinson – Tom's wife; as an object of prejudice she cannot find work

Mr Link Deas – owner of cotton-picking farm; offers Tom and Helen Robinson work and support

Mr Underwood – owner, editor and printer of the *Maycomb Tribune*

Mr Dolphus Raymond – white man from a rich family who lives with a black woman and their children; the white community look down on him as he seems permanently drunk, but Scout and Dill learn that by this he is giving the white community a reason for his chosen way of life

Mr Gilmer – the solicitor representing Mayella Ewell

Mrs Grace Merriweather – prominent, devout figure of the Maycomb Missionary Circle; organiser of the pageant

Mrs Farrow – another member of the Missionary Circle

Misses Tutti and Frutti Barber – old, deaf Maycomb sisters

Mrs Creshaw – town seamstress who makes Scout's pageant costume

Note that there are further characters mentioned, but that none of them have any significant action in the novel.

> **CHECKPOINT 38**
>
> In your opinion, are any of these minor characters actually major characters?

LANGUAGE AND STYLE

NARRATIVE STYLES

The style of *To Kill a Mockingbird* is comparable to nineteenth-century literature, much admired by Harper Lee. Similarities are:

- Full and leisurely portrayal of a particular community
- Attempt at **realism**
- Concern with the battle of good and evil
- Tragic and comic elements
- Sentimental feel, with a clear set of morals
- Chronological order of events (see **Structure**)

Some of its characteristics, for instance that it is a **regional novel**, link it to other twentieth-century Southern American writing as well as to traditional ideas of the nineteenth-century novel. It is of its time in its reference to history and exploration of contemporary concerns, for instance the theme of racial prejudice, which is still an important issue today.

HARPER LEE'S WRITING STYLE

As a writer with a legal background, careful organisation of written material comes 'with the territory'. Harper Lee has a clear, straightforward writing style and legal language permeates the novel. (Scout and Jem's language is similarly peppered with legal words, learned from their father and taken for granted.) However, Harper Lee also has the ability to conjure up atmosphere and create mystery and suspense in dramatic episodes, such as when Robert Ewell attacks the children.

CHECK THE FILM

Harper Lee's descriptions are vivid and cinematographic – one of the reasons, perhaps, why the novel has translated so well into film.

FIGURATIVE LANGUAGE

Harper Lee makes use of various stylistic devices to create effect. Scout talks about the characters she is describing in **similes**:

- Calpurnia's 'hand was as wide as a bed slat and twice as hard' (Ch. 1, p. 6)

- 'Jem's white shirt-tail dipped and bobbed like a small ghost dancing away to escape the coming morning' (Ch. 6, p. 63)

Simile is also used to create **images**, often recurring, to emphasise prominent ideas. The previous section on **Symbolism** shows how this is done with the mockingbird **motif**. Careful placing of images link up key themes and create a sense of coherence in the novel as a whole (see **Structure**).

Objects are **personified** by Scout which helps to reinforce a symbolic structure, for instance the description of Maycomb and the Radley Place in Chapter 1. The fence is referred to as 'a picket drunkenly guarding the front yard' (Ch. 1, p. 9) and the house 'droopy and sick' (Ch. 1, p. 16).

These examples and the use of **metaphors**, as well as illuminating meaning, evoke the traditions and ways of children growing up in the Southern United States. An example of this is the way Scout describes Atticus in court in Chapter 17 as going 'frog-sticking without a light' (p. 195), when she thinks that Atticus is starting something without the sufficient equipment to deal with it. Such childhood images are poetic in their naivety and originality, but have been crafted by a creative, grown-up narrator (Harper Lee).

HUMOROUS LANGUAGE

Figurative language like this lightens a story which is fairly tragic and depressing, and also helps to make the novel more realistic. Humorous use of language also has this effect, for instance Scout's malapropism when she has not understood the words 'absolute morphodite' (see **Glossary**, Chapter 8) and Robert Ewell's malapropism when, ironically he does not understand the meaning of 'ambidextrous' at the trial (see Glossary, Chapter 17).

SOUTHERN COLLOQUIALISMS AND DIALECT

Harper Lee's ability to capture a variety of dialect and southern colloquial expressions adds realism and authenticity to the novel. One example of a general southern colloquialism is 'buying cotton', a

CHECKPOINT 39

Find a **simile** in the text to describe Miss Caroline in Chapter 2, Mrs Dubose in Chapter 11 and Mayella Ewell in Chapter 18.

EXAMINER'S SECRET

Don't just 'namedrop' literary terms. Make sure you comment on *how* the techniques are used and the effect they have.

polite way of saying that the person does nothing. Varieties of speech are often used to make a social comment about a character:

- Child dialogue and use of slang are notable. See Jem, Scout and Dill's conversation at the end of Chapter 1. The narrator is clearly skilled in capturing children's language, but she is not restricted to this as she tells her story from a mature perspective.

- Robert Ewell uses a crude, harsh language at the trial and refers to Mayella being raped, 'screamin' like a stuck hog' (Ch. 17, p. 190). This is a grotesque metaphorical comment and it shows what little love and respect he has for his daughter. His swear words in the trial work in turning us against this character.

- Mayella's dialect is equally broad, representing the uneducated white community. She takes offence to Atticus's address of 'Ma'am' and 'Miss Mayella' (Ch. 18, p. 200), showing us that she has not been exposed to politeness and does not recognise basic social conventions.

- Tom's dialect is also broad: 'I passed by yonder she'd have some little somethin' for me to do – choppin' kindlin', totin' water for her' (Ch. 19, p. 211). However, in contrast to Robert Ewell, Tom's dialect is softer. He calls Judge Taylor and Atticus 'suh' and 'Mr Finch', and is the voice of politeness.

- Calpurnia speaks 'coloured-folks' talk' and 'white-folks' talk' (Ch. 12, p. 139), reflecting her background and inherent ways (her grammar gets 'erratic' when she is angry) but also her current position and the lack of education in the black community.

- Atticus, mirroring his personality, speaks courteously, formally but straightforwardly.

DIFFERENT PURPOSES OF LANGUAGE

Harper Lee therefore cleverly uses a variety of language for different purposes:

- To create atmosphere
- To reveal character
- To create symbolic structure
- To support and enhance key themes
- To show authenticity

CHECKPOINT 40

Harper Lee seems to be implying that the language of the white community is desirable to the black people and that what prevents the black community speaking well is their lack of education (Chapter 12). What do you think about this? Does this attitude reflect the time when it was written?

- To provide information
- To make a social comment
- To provide humour or reveal irony

CHANGES IN LANGUAGE

Language is never static. Some of the words Harper Lee used have a different meaning in today's society. The language used to describe black people has changed. Harper Lee and characters like Atticus and Calpurnia referred to black people as 'Negroes' and 'coloured men/women'. Today the term 'black' is a more acceptable term of description for skin colour and the 'Negroes'' descendants would now be referred to as 'African-Americans'. People would rarely say/write 'the coloured man' today, perhaps because it was used to designate a separate legal group under Apartheid in South Africa. However, 'nigger', a bad word in the novel and still not generally used by white people, has begun to be used by black people to refer to themselves. Black people are using a word which white people cannot use and therefore claiming exclusive right of usage. They are not accepting the 'white' creation of how or how not to refer to black people, but they are inventing their own terminology. By doing this the black community are creating an insecurity amongst white people as to how to refer to them.

Another noticeable change in language and meaning is in reference to 'coming out'. This has taken on a specific meaning in recent years, but today's meaning and the meaning in the novel are nevertheless linked. Boo's 'coming out' involves him revealing his true person to the condemning outside world and today's usage involves a person no longer shutting away their homosexual identity to a society which is less than accepting. Both have implications of fear, of being different, of making a bold statement by being known.

DID YOU KNOW?

The use of language in a novel locates it in a certain period. As you are reading, be aware of language that is now redundant or has a different meaning today.

PART FOUR

RESOURCES

HOW TO USE QUOTATIONS

One of the secrets of success in writing essays is the way you use quotations. There are five basic principles:

1 Put inverted commas at the beginning and end of the quotation.

2 Write the quotation exactly as it appears in the original.

3 Do not use a quotation that repeats what you have just written.

4 Use the quotation so that it fits into your sentence.

5 Keep the quotation as short as possible.

EXAMINER'S SECRET
There are different conventions for using double or single quotations. Check the accepted rules with your teacher and make sure you follow them in the exam.

Quotations should be used to develop the line of thought in your essays. Your comment should not duplicate what is in your quotation. For example:

> **Miss Maudie tells Scout that her father, Atticus, is the same in public as in private. She says, 'Atticus Finch is the same in his house as he is on the public streets'** (Ch. 5, p. 51)

Far more effective is to write:

> **Miss Maudie tells Scout that her father is the same person 'in his house as he is on the public streets'** (Ch. 5, p. 51)

However, the most sophisticated way of using the writer's words is to embed them into your sentence:

> **It seems likely that Robert Ewell not only beats his children but also sexually molests them, implied when Tom tells the court that Mayella told him that what she did with her father 'don't count'** (Ch. 19, p. 214)

When you use quotations in this way, you are demonstating the ability to use text as evidence to support your ideas – not simply including words from the original to prove you have read it.

COURSEWORK ESSAY

Set aside an hour or so at the start of your work to plan what you have to do.

EXAMINER'S SECRET

Check with your teacher the acceptable length of the essay.

- List all the points you feel are needed to cover the task. Collect page references of information and quotations that will support what you have to say. A helpful tool is the highlighter pen: this saves painstaking copying and enables you to target precisely what you want to use.

- Focus on what you consider to be the main points of the essay. Try to sum up your argument in a single sentence, which could be the closing sentence of your essay. Depending on the essay title, it could be a statement about a character: Mrs Dubose is one of the most courageous characters in *To Kill a Mockingbird*, as she carries out her decision to give up morphine, even though she is in a bed of pain; an opinion about setting: Maycomb court-house represents all that the white man's world stands for; or a judgement on a theme: I consider that the main theme of *To Kill a Mockingbird* is prejudice. Most of the characters within the novel experience prejudice from others and are, to some degree, prejudiced towards others.

- Make a short essay plan. Use the first paragraph to introduce the argument you wish to make. In the following paragraphs develop this argument with details, examples and other possible points of view. Sum up your argument in the last paragraph. Check you have answered the question.

- Write the essay, remembering all the time the central point you are making.

- On completion, go back over what you have written to eliminate careless errors and improve expression. Read it aloud to yourself, or, if you are feeling more confident, to relative or friend.

If you can, try to type you essay, using a word processor. This will allow you to correct and improve your writing without spoiling its appearance.

SITTING THE EXAMINATION

Examination papers are carefully designed to give you the opportunity to do your best. Follow these handy hints for exam success:

BEFORE YOU START

EXAMINER'S SECRET

Always write a plan for every answer. It ensures you answer the question and stops you from waffling and repeating yourself. Also, if you run out of time, you may gain marks from notes in the plan.

- Make sure you know the subject of the examination so that you are properly prepared and equipped.

- You need to be comfortable and free from distractions. Inform the invigilator if anything is off-putting, e.g. a shaky desk.

- Read the instructions, or rubric, on the front of the examination paper. You should know by now what you have to do but check to reassure yourself.

- Observe the time allocation – and follow it carefully. If they recommend 60 minutes for Question 1 and 30 minutes for Question 2, it is because Question 1 carries twice as many marks.

- Consider the mark allocation. You should write a longer response for 4 marks than for 2 marks.

WRITING YOUR RESPONSES

- Use the questions to structure your response, e.g. question: 'The endings of X's poems are always particularly significant. Explain their importance with reference to two poems.' The first part of your answer will describe the ending of the first poem; the second part will look at the ending of the second poem; the third part will be an explanation of the significance of the two endings.

- Write a brief draft outline of your response.

- A typical 30-minute examination essay is probably between 400 and 600 words in length.

- Keep your writing legible and easy to read, using paragraphs to show the structure of your answers.

- Spend a couple of minutes afterwards quickly checking for obvious errors.

WHEN YOU HAVE FINISHED

- Don't be downhearted – if you found the examination difficult, it is probably because you really worked at the questions. Let's face it, they are not meant to be easy!

- Don't pay too much attention to what your friends have to say about the paper. Everyone's experience is different and no two people ever give the same answers.

IMPROVE YOUR GRADE

Consider the question:

> Do you think that *To Kill a Mockingbird* is a depressing or an optimistic novel?

What is the question asking you? This question is asking you to talk about the messages of the novel, the main theme of prejudice, and to discuss whether the main subject (Tom's trial) and outcome is depressing or optimistic.

- Use the question to help you structure your response:

  The first part of the essay will describe how the novel could be seen to be depressing; the second part will look at reasons it could be seen as optimistic; the third part will bring the discussion to a conclusion, summarising the main arguments and stating the feeling you came away with after reading the novel.

IMPROVING YOUR RESPONSE FROM A 'D' TO A 'C'

- Instead of just retelling the story, going through all the depressing incidents in the novel and then all the optimistic incidents and then stating what you believe is the prominent tone, try to give your opinions on the action and thread the examples from the story into a list of points you are making.

- Instead of making the point, '**Tom's death is depressing**' expand on your point, saying:

EXAMINER'S SECRET

When studying/ revising, identify some key quotations which may be used for a variety of possible essays.

After the trial, the events take on an even more depressing turn when Atticus announces 'Tom's dead' (Ch. 24, p. 259). He died while trying to escape from prison, even before Atticus has had a chance to appeal. The force of this horror is emphasised when Atticus goes to tell Tom's wife Helen and she falls to the ground 'like a giant with a big foot' (Ch. 25, p. 264).

• Instead of just putting in a list of quotations or examples one after the other, you can see from above that using them within a sentence to back up a point is far more impressive.

• Instead of using quotations from one part of the novel, see if you can remember detail from the whole text – your answer will be much more convincing.

• Instead of just noting that she falls to the ground 'like a giant with a big foot' if you can add that **'This simile is very poweful as the depressing shock of the situation would have seemed like this to Helen Robinson.'** This shows that you are able to comment on how the techniques create an effect.

EXAMINER'S SECRET
You can get top marks in an English examination with two sides of writing. There is no need to write reams and reams!

IMPROVING YOUR RESPONSE FROM A 'B' TO AN 'A'

• Instead of just drawing from the book, you could use your knowledge about the context in which it is written (see **Author and context**) to sympathise with the writer's limitations of its time:

It would have been unrealistic for Harper Lee to allow Tom to win the trial as it is 1930s Southern America where the black community is still very much a prejudiced class. It is still not long after the American Civil War of 1861–5 and their release from slavedom, and the Civil Rights Movement of the 1950s to pursue equal status with white people has not yet begun. Therefore, the fact that Tom is deemed 'guilty' cannot be seen as totally depressing, but just realistic and in keeping with the views of race at the time, as Atticus said at the end of the trial 'as simple as black and white' (Ch. 2, p. 224)

EXAMINER'S SECRET
Remember to add small embedded quotes to your argument!

You could also cite the Scottsboro trials (see **Author and context**) as a recent example for Harper Lee where black people have had unfair trials. This would have been very much in her mind when writing.

- Instead of just observing how Jem feels after the trial – for example 'Jem is upset after the trial' – you can show how you share his views and can empathise with his ideas:

  When Jem bursts into 'angry tears' (Ch. 22, p. 234) we can sympathise with his frustration at what was so blatantly an unfair 'guilty' verdict and his feeling of anti-climax after a long build-up of tension.

- Instead of just using references to illustrate the optimistic/depressive elements of the novel, you should present a coherent line of thought about the subject, with quotations to secure your argument:

  When Atticus talks to the children about the trial he uses ironic echoing of the trial words when he replies to Jem's outburst that you cannot find a man guilty on that sort of evidence. He says, '*You* couldn't, but *they* could and did' (Ch. 23, p. 243), as Mr Gilmer had fatally used with Tom at the trial by saying, '*You* felt sorry for *her*, you felt *sorry* for her?' (Ch. 19, p. 218) where Tom, a black man, mistakenly shows sympathy for a white woman – an admission a white jury of the time just would not be able to accept if they were to save their pride. Atticus's words serve to remind us of the trial, and by addressing these words to Jem add an optimistic note that perhaps Jem is following in his father's footsteps and will continue this struggle for equality in the future. There is a further optimistic note, a 'shadow of a beginning' (Ch. 23, p. 245) when Atticus explains to the children that not only did the jury take a few hours rather than a few minutes to reach the verdict as Mr Cunningham ...

- Instead of observing the literary techniques used by the author, you could show how the techniques she uses emphasise her theme (example of ironic echoing above). Another example would be:

EXAMINER'S SECRET

If you cannot choose between two questions, jot down a plan for each to help you decide – it may be that what appeared to be the most straightforward question is more difficult than you thought.

The position of the symbol that has been a motif throughout, right at the end of the novel when Scout admits that Boo going to court would be 'like shootin' a mockingbird' (Ch. 30, p. 304), emphasises that the author is trying to make an important, positive point.

- Make sure you present a strong introduction – outline and expand on the ideas above about what the question is asking you – and a strong conclusion:

EXAMINER'S SECRET

Don't fall into the trap of just recounting the story. Try to analyse and comment, compare and contrast.

Even though we have seen how the novel has its depressing overtones, it is not entirely depressing and we have to remember that it is a product of its time. Atticus's response to Scout's opinion about Boo ('he was real nice', Ch. 31, p. 309) right at the end of the novel – his maxim of standing in another's shoes or skin which has been repeated throughout – leaves the reader on an upbeat note: 'Most people are, Scout, when you finally see them' (Ch. 31, p. 309). This implies that breaking down those barriers of prejudice has not arrived yet, but that it is only a matter of time.

SAMPLE ESSAY PLAN

This essay plan will show you how to structure an essay and will provide you with some ideas on the following title. It is divided into six parts and the points below have been made in note form. This is only one possible plan. You may well have your own ideas.

> In what ways do Atticus Finch and Robert Ewell differ, and what do they have in common?

EXAMINER'S SECRET

Remember to support your arguments with quotations from the novel. In a typical examination essay you might use as many as eight quotations.

PART 1: INTRODUCTION

Both Atticus Finch and Robert Ewell live in Maycomb, Alabama. Describe their houses, their reputation in the community and going back several generations.

PART 2: FAMILY STRUCTURE AND EXAMPLE TO CHILDREN

Both wives are dead. Describe how they remember them, what care they provide for their children, the physical appearance of their children. Describe Atticus's love, respect and education in contrast to Robert Ewell's neglect and abuse.

PART 3: WORK AND PUBLIC EXAMPLE

Both men are objects of prejudice. Describe the men's jobs (or lack of!), what names Atticus is called when he represents Tom, but the Maycomb people's basic respect for him. Contrast Robert Ewell – no job and what happens when he gets one. Compare Atticus's public example with Robert Ewell's, in the streets and at the trial.

PART 4: LAW-BREAKING

Compare Atticus's law-abiding nature (e.g. making Scout go to school, wanting Jem to speak out in court after Robert Ewell is dead) in contrast to Robert Ewell (children truanting, illegal hunting, lying). Discuss how, at the end of the novel, Atticus decides to break the law and why he does this.

PART 5: CONCLUSION

Therefore Atticus is educated, polite, hard-working, responsible and Robert Ewell is the opposite of all these. However, both men are, to some degree, outsiders in the community as neither of them are entirely 'normal'. Lasting impression – Robert Ewell a coward, but Atticus shows great courage. Therefore, there are some superficial similarities but they are very different characters.

This essay would achieve an even higher mark if:

- You added quotations to back up your points.
- The location of the community was described and you said a little bit about how people were effected by the Economic Depression (see **Setting and background**).
- You discussed the difference between Atticus's and Robert's language in the court-room.
- You brought out the difference of class and background between the two men.

EXAMINER'S SECRET
If you are allowed to choose the question that you answer, take a moment to consider which question you feel most confident about answering and have most to say about.

- You identified which character we know Harper Lee favours from her writing and how she has not broken down the stereotype of the 'White Trash' lower class by her harsh portrayal of Robert Ewell.

EXAMINER'S SECRET

Always think about the question carefully and work out exactly what you are being asked to discuss.

FURTHER QUESTIONS

The following questions are common essay titles in examinations and for coursework assignments. Look back at the **How to use quotations** and **Improve your grade** sections and then attempt these essay questions as practice.

1 Why, do you think, did the writer call her novel *To Kill a Mockingbird*?

2 To tell the story the writer uses the voice of her central character. What are the effects of this technique?

3 Describe how Harper Lee portrays the black community in the novel.

4 How effectively does the film of *To Kill a Mockingbird* deal with the main themes of the novel?

5 'Harper Lee was so desperate to make the reader sympathise with Tom Robinson that she made him an idealised, unconvincing character.' Do you agree with this statement?

6 Choose one or two settings in the novel. Discuss how they reveal character.

7 Does Harper Lee merely describe, or does she criticise?

8 'A story about childhood.' True or false?

9 Discuss the changes in the relationship between Scout and Jem as the novel progresses.

10 Consider the effects on the author's writing of where and when she lived.

EXAMINER'S SECRET

Always write a plan for every answer. It ensures you answer the question and stops you from waffling and repeating yourself. Also, if you run out of time, you may gain marks from notes in the plan.

Literary Terms

alliteration relating to the texture or onomatopoeic nature of language; words which start with similar-sounding consonants coming close together in the text (so sometimes known as head-rhyme) e.g. Scout suggests a scheme to succeed. Assonance is its vowel equivalent

autobiography the story of the author's life

bildungsroman a novel which describes a character's development from childhood to maturity, focusing on their experience, education and identity

chronology events arranged in the correct sequence of time

colloquialisms ordinary everyday speech, using informal expression and grammar

dialect accent and vocabulary varying by region and social background

epigraph a heading or quotation that writers sometimes use at the beginning of their work as an indication of theme

figurative language elaborate (as distinct from plain) language. Commonly **metaphor** and **simile**

first-person narrative stories told by an 'I' figure who is directly involved. This contrasts to the 'omniscient narrator' where the storyteller knows all and stands outside the story

flashback a term borrowed from films. A sudden jump backwards in time to an earlier episode or scene in the story (see 'echoing' in foreshadowing)

foreshadowing close to the idea of prophesying, an instance or reference to an incident coming later in the text. A contrast to 'echoing' (looking backwards)

genre a type of literature, for instance poetry, drama, biography, fiction

imagery language which builds up a picture or image (e.g. by the use of **metaphor** or **simile**)

irony when what is said/written is opposite to what is meant

leitmotif see motif

malapropism confused, amusing, inaccurate use of long words, so called after Mrs Malaprop in Sheridan's play *The Rivals* (1775), who refers to another character as 'the very pineapple of politeness' instead of pinnacle (malaprop from the French phrase *mal* – English equivalent, inappropriate)

maxim a short, pithy statement proposing model human behaviour

metaphor something described as being something else and 'carrying over' its associations

motif a repeated theme, image or character which gives the work a symbolic structure. **Leitmotif** is a repeated phrase

onomatopoeia words which sound like the noise they describe e.g. cuckoo

personification a variety of **figurative language** where things or ideas are treated as if they were people, with human attributes and feelings

realism an 'accurate' description of things as they 'really' are in 'ordinary' life

regional novel an emphasis on particular geographical customs and speech which have a significant effect on the development of the novel

satire aggressive **irony**. A humorous attack on human or institutional imperfection. Characterised by a ridiculing of the morally doubtful or absurd by a witty comparison with the ideal, or at least the preferred

simile when one thing is said to be like another, always containing the words 'like' or 'as' and allowing a comparison with things that are similar

symbolism something simple which represents something else more complicated (often an idea or quality), e.g. a flag symbolising national identity

CHECKPOINT 1 By referring to 'When enough years had gone by' and 'events leading up to his accident' (Ch. 1, p. 3) we know that it is the events of the past which make up the story.

CHECKPOINT 2 Atticus – for instance he has taught her to read.

CHECKPOINT 3 In contrast to Chapter 1 where we see Atticus treating his children as individuals, Miss Caroline's educational methods appear to make no room for the individual.

CHECKPOINT 4 It allows the reader to be presented with background information on the Ewell's poverty and their status within the community.

CHECKPOINT 5 They are effective because they force the children to think how they would feel if they were in Boo's position. This reminds us of when Atticus talks to Scout in Chapter 3 and tells her 'You never really understand a person until you consider things from his point of view' (p. 33).

CHECKPOINT 6 Mr Nathan Radley blocks the hole so that Boo cannot leave presents with the children anymore – so that he can have no contact with the outside world.

CHECKPOINT 7 The gift of the flower shows that Mrs Dubose has forgiven Jem his action, and also signifies that she is at last at peace and he will no longer have to serve his punishment.

CHECKPOINT 8 It allows the reader to learn about these episodes directly, and therefore the information is immediate and has not been filtered through Scout's eyes.

CHECKPOINT 9 The incident with the mad dog symbolises Atticus lashing out at madness (prejudice) to protect his community.

CHECKPOINT 10 Scout and Jem are confused because this is not characteristic of Atticus's way of speaking. He never tries to make Scout and Jem feel that they are superior in any way, but tries to

make them look at other people as equals with their own values and perspectives.

CHECKPOINT 11 Again the eavesdropping technique is used by the author to get information directly to the reader through Scout.

CHECKPOINT 12 Atticus says that the children made Walter Cunningham stand in Atticus's shoes for a moment.

CHECKPOINT 13 Tom's words are a big mistake, because such was the nature of prejudice at that time it would not have been acceptable by much of the white community for a black man to feel sorry for a white woman – in Mr Gilmer's retort he implies how ludicrous it is for a black man to feel sorry for a white woman under any circumstance. The white community therefore immediately turns against him, wanting him punished for his perceived arrogance.

CHECKPOINT 14 Atticus is not only saying that the outcome of the trial should be obvious by the evidence – that Tom Robinson is innocent – but suggesting that it will be decided on by people's prejudice about 'black' and 'white' and thus the outcome will be solely determined by the colour of Tom's skin.

CHECKPOINT 15 You will need to read carefully through Chapters 17–21 and jot down points in Mr Gilmer vs Atticus and Mayella vs Tom lists. If possible, do this with a friend so that you can compare your points.

CHECKPOINT 16 The 'perpetrated fraud' (note Scout's legal use of language!) is that Dolphus Raymond does not drink whisky out of his paper sack, as he leads people to believe. It is in fact Coca-Cola.

CHECKPOINT 17 Jem's views on the four kinds of people in Maycomb County is 'There's the ordinary kind like us and the neighbours, there's the kind like the Cunninghams out in the woods, the kind like the Ewells down at the dump, and the Negroes' (Ch. 23, p. 249). Scout however believes 'there's just one kind of folks. Folks' (Ch. 23, p. 250). Consider what you think – the strings to this argument could get complicated, so have some clear arguments with evidence to back up your opinions.

CHECKPOINT 18 This reminds us of Mr Gilmer's comment earlier. Find this comment and compare the two.

CHECKPOINT 19 Atticus is again trying to get the children to see things from another's point of view. You should now have a note of several times when he has asked the children to stand in a character's shoes or skin.

CHECKPOINT 20 See the discussion of the mockingbird motif in the section on **Symbolism** in **Themes**.

CHECKPOINT 21 Compare this scene to some where Scout is present. Perhaps you think it is not as fresh and immediate – or maybe you think the narrative works well using a variety of different techniques. Back up your answer with examples from the text.

CHECKPOINT 22 Find examples of what the judge said to Robert Ewell at the trial which might have made him feel foolish.

CHECKPOINT 23 They are both authors/narrators and both concerned with Maycomb County. They are both creating a pageant!

CHECKPOINT 24 Jem's arm being broken in the struggle.

CHECKPOINT 25 It makes us feel more sympathetic to Aunt Alexandra. Such traits make characters more than two-dimensional characters, so that they are not just flat good and bad characters but are more complex.

CHECKPOINT 26 As Jem is an innocent harmed, and has an outward injury similar to that of Tom's, he could also be linked to the mockingbird theme.

CHECKPOINT 27 Yes, several incidents have prepared us: hiding the presents, leaving Jem's trousers on the fence, putting a blanket around Scout's shoulders.

CHECKPOINT 28 One obvious example where the reader understands what is going on better than Scout is when the children go to find Atticus and the mob outside the Maycomb gaol. However, there are several other examples you could come up with.

CHECKPOINT 29 One example of Scout and Dill's naivety is at the end of Chapter 14 where they lie in bed and talk about where babies come from.

CHECKPOINT 30 Although Aunt Alexandra is arguably a prejudiced and difficult character, coming to live with the family when Atticus is involved in such a controversial trial could be seen as a very brave act.

CHECKPOINT 31 Thinking about the setting and background to the novel (see **Part One** of these Notes) and the strong messages Harper Lee makes, it could be considered a very courageous novel. Think about how.

CHECKPOINT 32 By emotional blackmail – crying for instance.

CHECKPOINT 33 Mr Dolphus Raymond is not seen as an individual as he is married to a black woman and is part of the black community. Nor is Tom seen as an individual. His unfair conviction is because he is part of a group – the black community.

CHECKPOINT 34 Two examples are Chapter 3 (p. 33) and Chapter 16 (p. 173). You should find several more. Compare your findings with a friend.

CHECKPOINT 35 Possibly not. At different periods it may be more or less acceptable to stereotype a certain 'type'. Stereotying a poor, lower-class man may now be considered politically incorrect – but this is an issue open for discussion and you may have different views.

CHECKPOINT HINTS/ANSWERS

CHECKPOINT 36 Because many threads would have been left hanging, for instance the children's game with the mystery of Boo Radley. Also it would be ending the novel on a very depressing and downbeat note.

CHECKPOINT 37 Depending on your argument, you should use examples to show that you think the two stories are separate and stand very much alone, or examples to show that the stories are linked in several different ways by their contrasts.

CHECKPOINT 38 This is obviously a matter of personal opinion, but some of the characters who you think have a major impact or presence, for example Mr Gilmer, Judge Taylor or Mr Dolphus Raymond, you could argue to be more significant than some others.

CHECKPOINT 38 Miss Caroline 'looked and smelled like a peppermint drop' (Ch. 2, p. 18). Mrs Dubose's mouth was 'like a clam hole at low tide' (Ch. 11, p. 119). Mayella Ewell is 'like a steady-eyed cat with a twitchy tail' (Ch. 18, p. 199).

CHECKPOINT 40 This is definitely reflective of that time. In many integrative societies a distinction will not be clearly drawn. Some groups of black people today will pride themselves on their distinctive dialect, not wishing to acquire 'white people's' language.

Test answers

Test Yourself (Chapters 1–11)

1 Scout (*Chapter 1*)

2 Scout (*Chapter 5*)

3 Atticus (*Chapter 3*)

4 Jem (*Chapter 1*)

5 Miss Maudie (*Chapter 5*)

6 Boo Radley (*Chapter 1*)

7 Anyone who shows courage e.g. Mrs Dubose, Atticus (*Chapter 11*)

Test Yourself (Chapters 12–21)

1 Mr Gilmer (*Chapter 19*)

2 Miss Maudie (*Chapter 16*)

3 Lula May (*Chapter 12*)

4 Robert Ewell (*Chapter 17*)

5 Dolphus Raymond (*Chapter 16*)

6 Aunt Alexandra (*Chapter 13*)

7 Mayella (*Chapter 19*)

Test Yourself (Chapters 22–31)

1 Jem (*Chapter 23*)

2 Heck Tate (*Chapter 30*)

3 Mrs Merriweather (*Chapter 24*)

4 Miss Gates (*Chapter 26*)

5 Atticus (*Chapter 22*)

6 The black people in the community (*Chapter 22*)

7 The white people in the jury (*Chapter 23*)

8 Boo Radley (*Chapter 29*)

NOTES

NOTES

Maya Angelou
I Know Why the Caged Bird Sings

Jane Austen
Pride and Prejudice

Alan Ayckbourn
Absent Friends

Elizabeth Barrett Browning
Selected Poems

Robert Bolt
A Man for All Seasons

Harold Brighouse
Hobson's Choice

Charlotte Brontë
Jane Eyre

Emily Brontë
Wuthering Heights

Shelagh Delaney
A Taste of Honey

Charles Dickens
David Copperfield
Great Expectations
Hard Times
Oliver Twist

Roddy Doyle
Paddy Clarke Ha Ha Ha

George Eliot
Silas Marner
The Mill on the Floss

Anne Frank
The Diary of a Young Girl

William Golding
Lord of the Flies

Oliver Goldsmith
She Stoops to Conquer

Willis Hall
The Long and the Short and the Tall

Thomas Hardy
Far from the Madding Crowd

The Mayor of Casterbridge
Tess of the d'Urbervilles
The Withered Arm and other Wessex Tales

L.P. Hartley
The Go-Between

Seamus Heaney
Selected Poems

Susan Hill
I'm the King of the Castle

Barry Hines
A Kestrel for a Knave

Louise Lawrence
Children of the Dust

Harper Lee
To Kill a Mockingbird

Laurie Lee
Cider with Rosie

Arthur Miller
The Crucible
A View from the Bridge

Robert O'Brien
Z for Zachariah

Frank O'Connor
My Oedipus Complex and Other Stories

George Orwell
Animal Farm

J.B. Priestley
An Inspector Calls
When We Are Married

Willy Russell
Educating Rita
Our Day Out

J.D. Salinger
The Catcher in the Rye

William Shakespeare
Henry IV Part 1
Henry V
Julius Caesar

Macbeth
The Merchant of Venice
A Midsummer Night's Dream
Much Ado About Nothing
Romeo and Juliet
The Tempest
Twelfth Night

George Bernard Shaw
Pygmalion

Mary Shelley
Frankenstein

R.C. Sherriff
Journey's End

Rukshana Smith
Salt on the snow

John Steinbeck
Of Mice and Men

Robert Louis Stevenson
Dr Jekyll and Mr Hyde

Jonathan Swift
Gulliver's Travels

Robert Swindells
Daz 4 Zoe

Mildred D. Taylor
Roll of Thunder, Hear My Cry

Mark Twain
Huckleberry Finn

James Watson
Talking in Whispers

Edith Wharton
Ethan Frome

William Wordsworth
Selected Poems

A Choice of Poets

Mystery Stories of the Nineteenth Century including The Signalman

Nineteenth Century Short Stories

Poetry of the First World War

Six Women Poets